Through the Year

THROUGH THE YEAR
An assembly book for the 1990s

W J Wilcock

© W J Wilcock 1990

The right of W J Wilcock to be identified as author of this work has been asserted by him in accordance with the Copyright, Designs and Patents Act 1988.

All rights reserved. No part of this publication may be reproduced or transmitted in any form or by any means, electronic or mechanical, including photocopying, recording or any information storage and retrieval system, without permission in writing from the publisher or under licence from the Copyright Licensing Agency Limited. Further details for such licences (for reprographic reproduction) may be obtained from the Copyright Agency Limited, of Tottenham Court Road, London W1P 9HE

First published in 1990 by
Basil Blackwell Ltd

Reprinted in 1992 and in paperback in 1994 by
Simon & Schuster Education

Reprinted in 1995 by
Stanley Thornes (Publishers) Ltd
Ellenborough House
Wellington Street
CHELTENHAM GL50 1YD
England

A catalogue record for this book is available from the British Library.

ISBN 0 7487 2373 0

Typeset in 10/12pt Times Roman
by Photo-graphics
Printed in Great Britain by
T. J. Press (Padstow) Ltd, Padstow, Cornwall

To: Joan, Andrew and Jennifer

Contents

Foreword   x

YEAR 1

Autumn term
Week 1	Sand castles	2
Week 2	Good luck!	3
Week 3	Jumbled words	5
Week 4	Signals	7
Week 5	Seeds	8
Week 6	Promises	9
Week 7	Excuses	10
Week 8	Saints	12
Week 9	Fireworks	14
Week 10	Remember	16
Week 11	Happiness	17
Week 12	Magnifying glass	19
Week 13	Albert's birthday	20
Week 14	Christmas customs	22
Week 15	Carol service	24

Spring term
Week 1	New Year's resolutions	25
Week 2	Choices	26
Week 3	Colours 1	27
Week 4	Colours 2	29
Week 5	Hands	31
Week 6	A round tuit	33
Week 7	Doors	35
Week 8	Castles	37
Week 9	No answer?	38
Week 10	Bill Stickers	40
Week 11	Crooked sixpence	42
Week 12	Twice my own!	43
Week 13	April fool!	45

Summer term
Week 1	Good news	46
Week 2	Cricket	47
Week 3	Hallmarks	48

Week 4	At sixes and sevens	50
Week 5	Sailing	52
Week 6	Cold shoulder	53
Week 7	Sand experiment	54
Week 8	Trivial pursuit	56
Week 9	Rust	57
Week 10	Up to scratch	58
Week 11	Sport	60
Week 12	Cheque books	61

YEAR 2

Autumn term

Week 1	Fred	64
Week 2	Flags 1	65
Week 3	Flags 2	69
Week 4	Ants	70
Week 5	What Tommy owes	71
Week 6	Shoelaces	73
Week 7	Horseshoe nail	75
Week 8	Jigsaws	76
Week 9	It's a changing world	78
Week 10	Road signs	80
Week 11	Time	83
Week 12	Names 1	85
Week 13	Names 2	87
Week 14	Weather forecasts	89
Week 15	Santa	91

Spring term

Week 1	Janus	93
Week 2	Thin ice	94
Week 3	Maths 1	96
Week 4	Maths 2	99
Week 5	Sine cera	101
Week 6	'Careless talk costs lives'	103
Week 7	'Dig for victory'	104
Week 8	What's my line?	105
Week 9	Listen!	107
Week 10	Flour grader	108
Week 11	If	109
Week 12	Good memories	111
Week 13	The greatest	113

Summer term
Week 1	Easter eggs	114
Week 2	It's not cricket	115
Week 3	Gilbert and Sullivan	116
Week 4	Wedding invitation	118
Week 5	God is now here!	120
Week 6	Donkeys	122
Week 7	Help!	124
Week 8	Snakes and ladders	125
Week 9	Beware the camel's nose	127
Week 10	A flash in the pan	129
Week 11	Jewels	130
Week 12	Motorway ends	131

SUPPLEMENT		135
1	Harmony	135
2	The big fight	136
3	Trees	137
4	Water	138
5	Disasters	139
6	Red spot	141
7	Lost property	142
8	Ice buns	143
9	Pied Piper	144
10	Maths 3	145
11	Be worth your salt	147
12	Fog	148

PRAYERS	150
INDEX	157

Foreword

The 1988 Education Act requires that schools provide a daily act of collective worship of a 'broadly Christian' nature. The emphasis in this book of assemblies is on Christian teaching, but most of the themes and topics will be appropriate to multi-faith communities and can easily be adapted to suit different schools. Many of the assemblies include a general theme or 'moral', together with a specifically Christian application, which forms part of the conclusion. Colleagues from other faiths, or those who teach in a multi-faith situation should, therefore, find most of the material in the book suitable for their needs. Where assemblies focus on particular Christian occasions or teachings, the presenter could select an alternative from the *Supplement* at the end of the book.

In compiling *Through the year* I have drawn on 35 years'experience as a teacher and head of a lower secondary school, and a lay preacher in many different denominations. The majority of themes included are original, though in a few cases I have taken familiar themes, presenting them in a new and interesting way which will be appropriate for lower secondary pupils. Each assembly contains all the material required by teachers: a story or talk; suggestions for visual aids; prayers, Bible readings and suggested hymns. The two parts of the book are arranged so that one assembly theme is provided for each week of the school year.

W J Wilcock

Year 1

Sand castles   WEEK 1

Introduction Welcome to a new school or new year group
Aim   To show the need for good foundations
Visual aid   (For younger pupils) Picture or photograph of a seaside scene.

Our theme today is 'making good foundations'. Many of you will have been to the seaside again for your summer holiday. When you were younger, I expect you made sandcastles on the beach. Can you remember the excitement of building castles near the water's edge and seeing what happened when the tide came in? Before long all traces of your castle were washed away. This is because they were built *out* of sand and built *on* sand. They did not have real foundations.

In some parts of Britain, such as Cromer on the Norfolk coast or the Birling Gap on the south coast there are houses built on the cliff edge which are falling into the sea because of coastal erosion or, in other words, poor foundations. Near Southport in Lancashire a school had to be pulled down and rebuilt because it was built on sandy ground and had poor foundations. But if you have visited Newquay in Cornwall you may have seen houses built on solid rock which for many years have withstood all that the raging sea, the wind and the storms could inflict. If you have been to Edinburgh you will have seen its famous castle, built prominently on a rock.

I hope that during this school year you will all do your best, that you will try hard and set about making good solid foundations upon which you can build in future years.

Christian application

Listen to what Jesus teaches us about the need to have good foundations.

Reading Matthew 7, 24–29 (It is recommended that you use the Revised Standard Version if possible.)
           The teachings of Jesus are the best foundations on which we can build our lives. These foundations will help us to withstand 'the storms of life'.
Prayer   No 10
Hymns   'Lord of all hopefulness'
           'The wise man built his house upon the rock'
           'Don't build your house on the sandy land'

Good luck! WEEK 2

Aim To show that life is not just a matter of luck, good or bad, and that God does guide and help people
Visual aids Drawings of a black cat, a horseshoe, a Number 13, a ladder

Are you superstitious? If you said 'No', think again. Do you have a lucky charm bracelet? Does your sport's team have a mascot? Would you walk under a ladder without turning a hair? Most of us like to think we're not superstitious. A neighbour once said to me 'I don't believe in luck. I'm not superstitious and no harm has come to me yet – touch wood!'

What do these objects have in common? (*Show drawings of cat and horseshoe.*)

Answer: They are supposed to bring good luck.

What do these objects have in common? (*Show drawings of No 13 and ladder.*)

Answer: They are supposed to bring bad luck.

It is very easy to blame 'luck' for the things that happen in our lives rather than taking responsibility for our own actions. If we do poorly in an examination, for example, we may complain about our 'bad luck' because the questions were so difficult – rather than admitting that we haven't prepared the work. How much better it is to develop qualities of determination and perseverance, rather than simply 'trusting to luck'.

Christian application

If we have faith in God we need never rely on 'luck'. We know that God loves and cares for us, so we should not believe in silly superstitions. Listen to what God says in this reading.

Reading Proverbs 3, 1–8 (It is recommended that the *Living Bible* is used for this reading, if possible.)
Prayer No 11
Hymns 'Now thank we all our God'
'All things bright and beautiful'
'God knows me'

Background information for the presenter

Tradition has it that, although it is unlucky for a black cat to cross our path, it is nevertheless lucky to actually own one. It is also said that if a black cat sneezes in the presence of the bride on her wedding morning then the marriage will be a happy one. Black cats have always been associated with witches and pagan supersitition but since Dick Whittington had a black cat and eventually became Lord Mayor of London it is thought by superstitious people that possessing a black cat brings the owner good luck.

As for horseshoes, these are supposed to be lucky because they are made of iron, a metal which traditionally gives protection from harmful spirits. The custom of attaching a horseshoe to the door of a house is connected with the instruction given to the children of Israel, when in captivity, to smear the lintel of the doorway with the blood of a lamb so that the angel of death would pass over that particular home.

Why is a number 13 said to be unlucky? This superstition dates back to the time of the last supper when there were 13 people present in the upper room, Jesus and the 12 disciples. Judus Iscariot was the thirteenth, the one who left the supper in order to betray Jesus. He later hanged himself.

There is a good deal of folklore attached to ladders. A dream about a ladder going upwards is said to bring good luck. The superstition probably originates in the story of the ladder which Jacob saw reaching to Heaven. Egyptologists conclude that the pyramids were built in steps in order to supply the dead Kings with a stairway to the heavens. Many people will not walk under a ladder simply because something might fall on them, or the ladder itself might collapse. A Christian rationalisation of this superstition is that to walk under a ladder would break the Holy Trinity symbolised by the triangle formed by ladder, wall and ground.

Jumbled words

WEEK 3

Aim To show that every member of the school (church) is important and has an important job to do

Visual aids Three posters/large sheets of paper, with the following well-known proverbs, jumbled up:
1 *Many hands make light work.*
2 *Too many cooks spoil the broth.*
3 *Every man to his own trade.*

This morning we'll begin by playing a game called 'jumbled words'. (*Show first poster.*) On this poster there is a well-known saying, but the words have all been mixed up. You have to try to put the words in the right order. Put up your hand as soon as you think you have done it.

Answer: Many hands make light work.

Think about this saying for a few moments. It means that a job of work is made much easier if a lot of people are involved, doing their share.

For example, it takes 20 painters, employed full-time, to paint Blackpool Tower, and they use 5.5 tons of paint! When they have completed the task they have to begin all over again, because by then the first part of the tower needs to be re-painted! If there were only five decorators doing the work, they would never get the job done.

Can you think of any jobs at school which would be very difficult and time-consuming for only a few pupils, but which soon get done if everyone shares in the work?

Here are two more sayings. Again the words have been jumbled up. Can you sort them out? (*Show posters 2 and 3.*)

Answers: Too many cooks spoil the broth.
Every man to his own trade.

What do you think these sayings mean? At home we can't all cook the meal (although it might be a good idea if we took turns). It is much better if each member of the family offers to do a different job. One may choose to peel the potatoes, another to cook the meal, another to set the table. Afterwards, it is very helpful if one clears the table, one washes up, one dries and another puts the dishes away.

In a school sports team, we can't all score the goals. A winning team needs players in attack and defence, a goalkeeper . . . In other words, each member has an important part to play to contribute to the success of the whole team. It's 'every person to his or her own trade'. We should all use our different abilities to the full to help the work of our school to be successful.

Christian application

God has given us a small part to play in trying to make the world a better place. We should all try to extend His kingdom of love. The more people help, the easier the task will be.

As we grow up, we should ask God to show us what special work He wants us to do.

Reading   Romans 12, 6–8
Prayer   No 15
Hymns   'At the name of Jesus'
             'Who is on the Lord's side?'
             'When I needed a neighbour'

Signals

WEEK 4

Aim　　　To give some guidelines for 'right living'
Visual aid　Model or picture of a set of traffic signals

How chaotic our roads would be if there were no traffic signals! How dangerous it is when motorists do not obey the signals we have! If a car fails to *stop* when the lights are on red a very serious accident could occur. When a driver does not move off as soon as the lights have changed to green the drivers behind may well start sounding their horns and become impatient, because of the delay caused. Every good driver knows that as soon as the lights turn to amber he or she must be *ready* to pull away when they turn to green.

In life, too, there are times when we should STOP. There are times when we should GO. And there are times when we should BE READY.

Christian application

In the Bible God sometimes tells us to STOP. Jesus said to his disciples: 'Don't worry about things – food, drink and clothes – your Heavenly Father already knows that you need them.' The message is clear. We should stop worrying, trust God and do our best.

God's traffic signals also tell us when to GO. Listen now to this familiar story which Jesus told.

Reading　　The Parable of the Good Samaritan – Luke 10, 25–37 (It is recommended that you use the RSV.)

In this story the traveller had been attacked by robbers and had been left to die. When he saw the priest come along, he must surely have thought help was on its way, but he passed by on the other side of the road. The same thing happened with the Levite. It was the Samaritan who showed kindness and compassion and was willing to help the man who had been attacked. Jesus said that we should be prepared to *Go* and do the same, that is be willing to help others in need and show them kindness. We must all *Be ready* to behave like this.

Prayer　　No 13
Hymns　　'Who is on the Lord's side?'
　　　　　　'Forth in thy name O Lord I go'
　　　　　　'Be bold, be strong'

Seeds WEEK 5

Aim To illustrate how great things can grow from small beginnings
Visual aid Matchbox full of seeds

Put up your hand if you can guess what is in this matchbox.

It contains seeds; 360 seeds in fact, and they are wheat seeds. This morning I want to tell you about a very interesting experiment with a matchbox full of wheat seeds. It was carried out by the Rev Clifton Robinson, an American minister. Clifton Robinson planted the contents of a matchbox full of wheat seeds just like this. When the wheat grew he watered it and cared for it, until it was ripe. Then he harvested the crop, but he kept the ears of wheat to plant again for the next year's harvest. This he did for six successive years, not using the crop to make bread but instead re-planting the seeds. By the sixth harvest, Rev Robinson's field of wheat covered 2,666 acres and yielded 66,560 bushels of corn. This time the corn was made into bread – 2,282,000 loaves which, if laid end to end would have stretched 150 miles (that's the distance from [Stoke] to London). All this had happened in just six years, from one matchbox full of seeds.

This story shows how great things can grow from small beginnings. Never think that you are too small or unimportant to do anything worthwhile. We can all work to make the world a better place.

Christian application

Rev Robinson planted the wheat, cultivated it and harvested it. But God provided the life, rain and sun without which there could be no harvest Jesus told a story about a tiny mustard seed which grew into a great tree:

Reading Matthew 13, 31,32
No matter how insignificant our talents seem to be, God can use them to help carry out his great plans.
Prayer No 24
Hymns 'We plough the fields and scatter'
'Thank you for every new good morning'
'Colours of the day'

Promises

WEEK 6

Aim To show the need to keep our promises
Visual aid A £5 note

Promises! We are all good at making promises, but are we good at keeping them? Some people make very vague promises. I know one young man who left home to start work and wrote home to his mother: 'Dear Mum, I am sending you fifty pounds, but not this week!'

Sometimes people make promises which are so rash that they could not possibly keep them. I have in my possession a piece of paper upon which someone has written me a promise. I will be very cross if that person breaks his promise. The promise is this 'I promise to pay the bearer on demand the sum of five pounds'. It has been signed by the Chief Cashier of the Bank of England. The paper itself has no value at all, but because it has been signed it is worth goods to the value of five pounds. This is a promise which is always kept. He is as good as his word. Are we?

Christian application

There is someone who makes even greater promises. I mean God himself. He promises that if we say we are sorry He will always forgive us (see 1 John 1, 9). And He promises to help us if we trust Him. In fact, the Bible is full of promises God has made. (For examples, see Matthew 18, 20; Romans 8, 28; 2 Corinthians 12, 9; John 10, 28; Matthew 28, 20.)

Our reading tells of two sons who were asked to do an important job by their father. One of them did not keep his promise.

Reading Matthew 21, 28–31a
Prayer No 17
Hymn 'O Jesus I have promised'

Excuses

WEEK 7

Aim To show that we must face up to our responsibilities
Reading The parable of the great supper. Luke 14, 16–24
'They all alike began to make excuses'.

What a feeble excuse the first man gave. No-one in his right mind would buy some land without first checking that it was either good firm gound, suitable to build on OR good rich land suitable to cultivate.

The second man's excuse was no better. To buy ten oxen without first checking that they were strong and healthy would be very stupid – like buying a second hand car without inspecting it and having a test drive!

You may think that the third person had a reasonable excuse. But not so! If this man had *really* wanted to go to the banquet, would his wife have stopped him? Apparently in those days people were all too ready to make excuses. You would never make excuses – would you? Or do you recognise the following?

(*A group of pupils could perform the following sketch.*)

Sketch

Teacher Now, 1A, I want you to put your homework books on my table.

Narrator And they all alike began to make excuses!

Pupil 1 I left my book on the table at home.

Pupil 2 My mother must have taken my book out of my bag.

Pupil 3 I didn't have a pen so I couldn't do my homework.

Pupil 4 The dog chewed my book!

Pupil 5 I didn't have time to do my homework because I had to go out at 7.30.

Pupil 6 I wasn't able to do my homework because I only got in at 7.30.

Pupil 7 The baby was sick on it!

Pupil 8 My little brother scribbled on it.

Pupil 9 My Uncle Joe visited us from Australia and I was so excited I forgot to do my homework.

Things haven't changed much since Jesus' time, have they? People are just as ready to make excuses – often very silly ones! We can usually see through other people's excuses – but we don't expect them to see through ours.

In the parable Jesus told, the ones who made excuses missed the chance of going to a banquet. Their places were given to others. If we make excuses, we risk losing out – there are always others ready to step in and benefit.

Christian application

We can never make excuses to God.

Prayer No. 14
Hymns 'God intrusts to all, talents few or many'
'God knows me'

Saints WEEK 8

Aim To explain the significance of Halloween and All Saints Day
Visual aid Halloween items and pictures, for example turnip lanterns, witches, broomsticks

Today I'm going to talk to you about witches, broomsticks, black cats, magic spells, skeletons, ghosts – and SAINTS!

Are you going to a Halloween party this year? It can be a lot of fun to dress up as witches and ghosts, to make lanterns and play Halloween tricks and games. But what does Halloween mean?

Every day when we say the Lord's Prayer in Assembly we say 'Hallowed be Thy Name'. This means that God's name is to be honoured and respected. In the Christian church throughout the ages there have been people who have led very good lives, serving God and being helpful and kind to others. The Church calls these people 'Saints'. Saints were, at first, called 'Hallows' because they were especially honoured and respected. Some Saints have a special day, eg

    Saint George (the patron saint of England) April 23rd
    Saint Andrew (the patron saint of Scotland) November 30th
    Saint David (the patron saint of Wales) March 1st
    Saint Patrick (the patron saint of Ireland) March 17th

Do you know of any other saints? Perhaps you have heard of Saint Christopher – the patron saint of travellers; Saint Cecilia – the patron saint of musicians; or Saint Francis – the patron saint of animals.

There are many many saints, too many for each to have a special day. So we remember them all on All Saints Day or, as it is also called, All Hallows.

The day before All Hallows was called All Hallows' Eve, and this name gradually changed to Hallowe'en. Hundreds of years ago people believed in evil spirits, ghosts, witches and black magic. They thought that these evil things would not dare to do any mischief on All Hallows Day, so they woud be very active the day before, Hallowe'en, to make up for it. To frighten these evil spirits away, superstitious people used to build bonfires and make masks and lanterns. Of course, today we know that there are no evil spirits, but we still carry on the old customs just for fun!

So what is a Saint? This question was once asked by a Sunday School teacher and one of the children in her class replied 'A Saint is someone the light shines through'. She was thinking of a stained-glass window she had seen in church with the sunshine pouring through it. But she was right in another sense too. Ordinary people like you and me can be 'Saints' if we allow God to use us and shine his light, his love, his way of life through us.

Reading   Philippians 1, 27–30
           (Paul is writing to the Saints in the early church.)
Prayer   No 25
Hymns   'For all the Saints'
          'Heavenly Father may thy blessing'
          'Jesus bids us shine'

Fireworks

WEEK 9

Theme   The sort of people we should try to be
Visual aids   A poster advertising fireworks *or* several specimens (stored in a tin box) *or* some used firework cases collected from the previous year

Remind the children of the firework code:

- Get an adult to set off the fireworks and stand well clear.
- Don't hold a lighted firework in your hand unless it clearly states that it is safe to do so.
- Don't return to a firework which you have tried to light if it has not gone off.
- Keep fireworks in a tin box.
- Don't wear wellington boots on bonfire night.
- Don't wear coats/anoraks with loose hoods.

Whenever possible, it is much better to attend an organised firework display.

There are all sorts of different fireworks. There are all sorts of different people! In fact, some people are rather like fireworks. Let me give you some examples:

1. Do you recognise this firework? It is a banger. Bangers make a lot of noise, irritate and generally annoy people. Does this sound like some boys and girls you have come across?
2. Next we have a rocket! Light the touch paper and quickly stand back as it soars into the air. I know some people like this rocket – they have very short tempers. At the slightest provocation they 'go up into the air'.
3. Here's a Catherine Wheel. This one goes round and round – but it doesn't get very far! Some people are so disorganised that they seem to go round and round in circles. They never get anywhere and they don't achieve very much.
4. Finally – look at this group of fireworks (*show examples such as Chrysanthemum Fountain; Silver Cascade; Golden Rain; sparklers*). These are the ones which fill the place with light and give pleasure to everyone.

Which sort of firework would you most like to be? The world might be a better place if we were all like sparklers and tried to spread happiness and pleasure among the people we meet.

Christian application

What is it that makes fireworks different? Is it just the shape of the case? Just the colour of the outside wrapping? Not really. It is what is inside that matters; the mixture of chemicals inside the firework determines whether it makes a lot of noise or gives beauty and pleasure. This is true with people too. It is what they are like *inside* that matters. Jesus tells us to 'let our light shine'. (See also Ephesians 3, 17 and 1 Corinthians 6, 19.)

Reading Matthew 5, 14–16
Prayer   No 3
Hymn   'Let us with a gladsome mind'
          'Go tell it on the mountain'

Remember

WEEK 10

Theme Training one's memory
Visual aid Remembrance Day poppy or poppy wreath. Checklist

Do people ever say to you: 'You'd forget your head if it wasn't screwed on'?

Some boys and girls have a great difficulty in remembering things. It can be a good idea to have a checklist like this. (*Show ready-made checklist, or write one up on a board/flipchart.*)

Things I must remember

1 My dinner money
2 My tie
3 My school books
4 My pen, pencil, ruler, rubber
5 My games kit
6 My cookery/woodwork apron

We must also remember to be polite, tidy, kind and helpful.

At this time of year we remember all the men and women who fought for their country in the two World Wars and in other wars. We remember, too, those who are still alive but continue to suffer from injuries they received in war. We buy our Remembrance Day poppies to support the charity which helps these people and their families. The poppy was chosen to remind us of one of the most terrible battles of the First World War, at a place called Flanders in Belgium, where the fields are covered with red poppies in summer.

We remember all these people in our prayers today.

Christian application

The Bible tells us to *remember* how good God is to us.

Reading Psalm 105, 4, 5
Prayer No 6 and/or No 8
Hymns 'O God our help in ages past'
'Heavenly Father, may thy blessing'

Happiness *WEEK 11*

Aim To show the source of true happiness
Visual aid A card with the Chinese word for 'happiness'

What do you think would make you really happy? Put up your hand if you would like to suggest some things.

> A new bicycle?
> Some new clothes?
> A big house?
> Good things to eat?
> Lots of friends?
> Being successful?

I know lots of people who have all these things but they don't seem very happy. They enjoy themselves from time to time but it doesn't seem to last.

The Chinese word on this chart says 'Happiness'. (I'm not going to attempt to pronounce it!)

Chinese is a picture language. The figure on the left is of a Chinaman, the top right-hand figure is the mouth of a Chinese boy or girl, and below is a picture of a Chinese rice field. Why does this mean happiness?

Traditionally, a Chinese person's idea of happiness is to be able to grow enough rice to feed all their children. This may not sound very exciting to you, but imagine how happy a bowl of rice would make someone who was starving (like the tragic victims of famine in . . . .). For many poor people, happiness is simply a matter of having enough to eat.

When was the last time you felt ill, or upset? Did your possessions make you feel any better? Lots of possessions cannot bring us happiness.

Christian application

Jesus talked about a different kind of happiness. He told his disciples that they could be happy even when things went wrong. Trusting in God can give us peace of mind, something far more important than having lots of possessions.

As you listen to this famous passage from the Sermon on the Mount, replace the word 'blessed' with the word 'happy'.

Reading Matthew 5, 1–12 (The Living Bible makes the meaning very clear)
Prayer No 19
Hymns 'O happy band of pilgrims'
'Happiness is to know the Saviour'
'I am so glad'
'If you want joy, real joy'

Magnifying glass

WEEK 12

Aim   To show how we can spread the good news
Visual aid   Magnifying glass

If you have read any Sherlock Holmes stories or seen them on television you will know that all good detectives have a magnifying glass.

The tiniest clue can be made large and clear with one of these. A thumb print becomes perfectly visible. The magnifying glass makes things seem several times bigger.

Our lives can be like magnifying glasses, too. When Mary received the news that she would have a baby who would be the Saviour of the World she was so thrilled that she exclaimed – 'My soul shall magnify the Lord'. She wanted so much to praise God and tell others of the good news that she magnified it and made it bigger for all to see.

We too should magnify the Lord by the way we live, by being helpful and kind. We should magnify the Lord in what we say, by telling others of the good news of His love for them at Christmas.

Reading   The magnificat. Luke 1, 46–55
Prayer   No 15
Carol   'Good Christian men rejoice'
          'Come and praise the Lord our King'

Albert's birthday WEEK 13

Aim To illustrate the true meaning of Christmas
Visual aids Two large greetings cards, with the following words:
Happy Birthday to Albert
Happy CHRISTmas

This is the story of Albert's birthday (*Show the first card.*) Albert was ten. He had only just moved to the district with his family and started at the local Junior School. Albert was anxious to make friends, so he invited all the members of his class to his birthday party that Saturday.

The great day arrived and one by one as the guests turned up at Albert's home, Albert's mother opened the door and showed the children to the room where the party was being held. Games were in full swing and everyone joined in with enthusiasm. They played all the games people usually play at parties. They ate all the things people usually eat at parties: sandwiches, crisps, sausage rolls, more crisps, jellies, cakes, trifle, ice cream – everything you could possibly wish for.

Eventually, however, all good things had to come to an end. As the guests were leaving, one by one, they thanked Albert's mother for providing such an enjoyable party.

At school the following Monday the classroom was buzzing. Everyone was talking about the party:

'Wasn't it a great party?' said Tom.
'We played some smashing games,' said Julie.
'Yes, we all had a great time at Albert's birthday par . . . at Albert's . . . at Al . . ., I say,' said Martin, 'I don't remember seeing Albert there!'
'Neither do I,' said Sandra, 'now that you come to mention it, I'm sure Albert wasn't there!'

Suddenly there was a great hush. Everyone was shocked. They had all been to Albert's birthday party and Albert himself wasn't there. No-one had noticed. No-one had missed him.

That story was made up! Of course nothing like that could ever happen, could it? But every year it does happen. In a few weeks' time it will be Christmas – the birthday of the Lord Jesus Christ. But many people will forget all about him.

(*Show the second card.*) How shameful to have the birthday of the Lord Jesus Christ and leave him out of the celebrations.

This Christmas time let us especially remember God's love to us in sending his son Jesus to be our Saviour.

Reading John 1, 1–12
Prayer No 5
Carols 'Love came down at Christmas'
'O little town of Bethlehem'
'The Virgin Mary had a baby boy'

22 Through the Year

Christmas customs   WEEK 14

Aim   To show the Christian significance of some customs which were originally pagan

Visual aids   Sprig of holly, sprig of mistletoe, Christmas presents, a decoration, candle, mince pie

A group of pupils could be rehearsed to present this assembly theme.

Introduction (1st pupil)
Have you done all your Christmas shopping? Wrapped the presents? Put up the Christmas decorations? Most of us get caught up in preparations for Christmas, but do you know how some of these traditions began?

Mistletoe (2nd pupil)
In the Middle Ages, superstitious people believed that spirits lived in the fields and woodlands. In the depths of winter they brought branches of evergreens and foliage into their homes, so that the spirits could keep warm. That's how the tradition of decorating our houses with evergreens began.

(*Show mistletoe*) Mistletoe is traditionally associated with love. The ancient Britons used mistletoe in their religious ceremonies. Christians have carried on this tradition. Mistletoe reminds us of God's love for us, and of the Christmas message that we must love each other.

Holly (3rd pupil)
In Scandinavian countries like Norway and Sweden, people call the holly tree the 'Christ-thorn' because it reminds them of the crown of thorns which Christ was made to wear as he was led away to be crucified. The red berries look like drops of blood.

Candles (4th pupil)
Before the days of electric lighting people did not have 'fairy lights' to decorate their Christmas trees, just coloured candles (*show candle*). This custom of having lights in the home goes back long before Christian times. Long ago, pagan people worshipped the sun. They thought that 25 December was the shortest day of the year. On that day, they lit torches and tapers in their homes to welcome the return of lighter and warmer days. We know now that the shortest day is 21 December, but Christians still celebrate the birth of Jesus, the 'Light of the World' on 25 December. For this reason they continue to decorate their homes with lights.

Decorations (5th pupil)
People who could not bring evergreens or foliage into their homes made imitation foliage out of paper. That was the start of Christmas decorations. Nowadays we decorate our homes with tinsel and paper decorations of every conceivable colour (*show decoration*).

Mince pies (6th pupil)
(*Show mince pie*) These were originally oval in shape. They reminded Christian people of the cradle in which the baby Jesus was placed. Some people make a wish when they eat a mince pie. Originally, Christians used to meditate silently and think of God's gift of the Christ-child.

Gifts (7th pupil)
As we give gifts to our friends and members of the family we should remember that the wise men started it all by bringing gifts of gold, frankincense and myrrh to the Christ-child. Remember, too, that Jesus himself teaches us that it is more blessed to give than to receive. In our prayer to-day we thank God for the greatest gift of all, without whom there would be no Christmas – the gift of Jesus Christ.

Prayer   No 22
Reading 1 John 4, 7–12 (or 21)
Carols   'Hark, the Herald Angels Sing'
          'See Him lying on a bed of straw'

Carol service (Taken by the pupils)   WEEK 15

1st pupil   As we worship God in our carol service we remember his love to us. He sent the gift of His Son Jesus Christ Our Lord. The first carol is *Once in Royal David's City*.

2nd pupil   First reading: The Birth of Jesus (Luke 2, 1–7)
The second carol is *O little town of Bethlehem*.

3rd pupil   Second reading: The Shepherds visit the manager (Luke 2, 8–20)
Now we will sing the carol *Unto us is born a Son*.

4th pupil   Third reading: The wise men come to worship Christ (Matthew 2, 1–12).

5th pupil   Prayers No 1, 5 and 22.

6th pupil   Our last carol is *O come, all ye faithful*.

           The grace

New Year's resolutions **WEEK 1**

Aim To provide suggestions for New Year's resolutions; to encourage us not to make the same mistakes we made last year

Happy New Year! Have you made any New Year's resolutions? At this time many people make promises to themselves about things they will do – or not do – in the year ahead. We think of those things in our lives which have not been up to standard, any mistakes we have made in the past or anything we have left undone and we resolve to be better in this new year. We promise ourselves that our work, our effort and our behaviour will improve in the future.

Here are some resolutions which members of form . . . . . have made. They will read them out for you. (*If it is not possible to get pupils' actual resolutions, you could use the following list.*)

Pupil 1 My New Year's resolution is to keep my bedroom tidy.
Pupil 2 My resolution is to clean my teeth twice a day.
Pupil 3 I promise to take my dog out for a walk every day instead of leaving it to my Dad.
Pupil 4 I am going to be more helpful at home by drying the dishes.
Pupil 5 I am going to try to be kind to my younger sister.
Pupil 6 I am going to eat more fresh fruit and not as many sweets.
Pupil 7 My resolution is to turn the television off when I do my homework.
Pupil 8 I am going to try not to lose my temper so often.

These are just a few suggestions for New Year's resolutions. It isn't too late for you all to make a resolution. The important thing is being determined to keep it.

Christian application

The best resolution we could make is to follow Jesus' example and teaching.

Reading Luke 2, 51, 52
Prayer   No 7
Hymns   'Jesus good above all other'
           'When Jesus walked in Galilee'

Choices WEEK 2

Aim Helping to make wise decisions and right choices
Visual aid Magazines such as *Which*, *Choice* or *What car?* Career pamphlet

The theme of our assembly is making decisions. Let's think about some of the decisions we have to make in the course of a day.

The first thing we do when we wake up is to make a decision – whether to get up or stay in bed and go back to sleep!

We then choose what to put on, what to have for breakfast . . . At school we may choose who to sit with and who to play with. All through the day we are constantly making decisions. It's just the same at home. Do you start your homework or watch TV? Will you stay in or go out?

Of course, these are all fairly minor decisions. We also have to make much more important choices, for example:

- which subjects to study
- which career to follow (*show career pamphlet*)
- which washing machine or car to buy (*show magazine*)
- where to live
- who to marry . . .

As we grow up we must learn to make wise, correct decisions.

Christian application

Joshua challenged the people of Israel to make a very important decision: whether or not to obey and follow God.

Reading Joshua 24, 14–18
Prayer No 25
Hymns 'O Jesus I have promised' (modern tune)
'He's got the whole world in His hands'

Colours 1   WEEK 3

Aim   To show how colours have different associations and to relate these to the pupils' experiences
Visual aids   Sheets of brightly-coloured red, yellow and green card

What is your favourite colour? Can you say why? Today we are going to think of colours and their significance. In particular we will consider three colours from which we can learn important lessons: red, yellow and green.

  1 The colour RED is used to warn of danger (think of fire engines and road warning signs). It is also a sign of anger. If someone gets into a real rage they may say 'I saw red' – they were so blinded by fury that they didn't know what they were doing. As a result, they might damage something or hurt someone.

  2 YELLOW can be associated with cowardice.

(Short sketch)
1st pupil: 'Don't bother walking all the way to the crossing!'

2nd pupil: 'Remember what we were told at school – always use the zebra crossing.'

3rd pupil: 'Come on quick, nip between these two lorries. Come on, don't be chicken – you're yellow!'

Have you ever been tempted to do something stupid like that? In fact, saying 'No' isn't cowardly. It takes much more courage to stand up for what you know is right and sensible, when others behave stupidly.

  3 We sometimes describe people as being GREEN with envy.

(Short Sketch)
1st pupil: 'Susan is always getting new clothes, I wish I could have some!'

2nd pupil: 'I wish my parents would buy me a new racer, like Julian's.'

3rd pupil: 'It's not fair, we can't afford to go abroad for our holidays like everyone else.'

4th pupil: 'It's not fair, Julie didn't deserve to get more marks in the examination than I did.'

Envy leads to many of the world's troubles. If people did not envy they would not steal other people's possessions; they would not break into or damage other people's cars; they would not break into other people's homes. Without envy there would be fewer wars and conflicts.

Christian application

Reading Romans 12, 9–18
 In this reading, Saint Paul tells us how Christians should live together without anger, cowardice or envy.
Prayer No 19
Hymn 'Heavenly Father, may Thy blessing'
 'Who put the colours in the rainbow?'

Colours 2   WEEK 4

Aim   To show how colours have different associations and to relate these to the pupils' experiences
Visual aids   Sheets of black, blue, silver, gold (and white) card

Here are some more colours for us to consider. Let us see what we can learn from them.

1. We associate the colour BLUE with cold. In fact we even say sometimes that we are blue with cold. None of us likes the sort of person who has a cold personality, who is unappreciative or who is aloof. We are much more likely to choose as our friends those who have a warm personality, those who are co-operative, helpful and kind.

2. BLACK is often associated with gloom, despair, disaster or wrong-doing. From time to time we all have days which are black, when everything seems to go wrong and everything seems to get on top of us. Do not despair – our next colour gives encouragement.

3. SILVER. You've probably heard people say 'Every cloud has a silver lining'. No matter how black things seem, there is always a glimmer of hope. Things will work out right if we persevere and always do our best.

4. GOLD. 'Silence is golden'. An important lesson we must learn as we grow up is when to speak up for ourselves, when to ask questions and when to remain silent. There are times when we should quietly get on with our work. Those who discover this secret are the ones who seem to get the best results. There are times when 'silence is golden'. If we are always causing a commotion and forever speaking out of turn, we don't leave any time to listen. No wonder we don't learn as much as we should.

Christian application

WHITE is the colour of purity. God wants us to be pure and good. But He knows that we are only human; we often fall short of His high standards. God promises that no matter how often we fail, He will forgive us if we are sorry. (See Psalm 51, 7; Isaiah 1, 18)

Reading　Ecclesiastes 3. 1–8
Prayer　No 11
Hymns　'All the beauty I behold over land and sea'
'For the beauty of the earth'
'Colours of the day'

Hands

WEEK 5

Aim   To encourage pupils to make the best use of their talents
Visual aids   Several outline diagrams of hands, including the presenter's

Everyone's hands are different. When you were younger did you ever try drawing around your own or someone else's hand?

Here are some hands which belong to people present in our assembly. (*Show outline hands and describe some aspect of each person, as in the following examples.*)

> These are the hands of a rugby player, they belong to . . . . .
> These belong to a member of the hockey team, they are . . . . . 's hands.
> These are the hands of the shooter for the netball team, they are . . . . . 's hands.
> These hands won the art competition, they belong to . . . . .
> These hands played in goal for the school football team and of course they belong to . . . . .

Can you guess to whom these hands belong? I will give you some clues. (*List a number of your/the presenter's attributes, as follows*)

> They can play the piano.
> They can write on the chalk board.
> They are good at gardening – they have got to be!
> They are good at washing up – they have got to be!
> They are good at tennis.
> They used to be good at badminton.
> They belong to the world's worst golfer!
> They once played in goal in a football match and let in five goals!

That's right! You have guessed. They are my hands.

  We are all different, just like our hands. And we all have different talents. No-one can be good at everything. You may be good at art, your best friend may be a fast sprinter. Whatever our talents, we must try to use them wisely and fully.

Christian application

In this story, which Jesus told, a 'talent' was a sum of money. Nowadays we think of talents as any God-given gift.

Reading   Matthew 25, 14–18.

Jesus went on to explain that the servants who received five talents and two talents and used them wisely were praised and rewarded. But the servant who made no attempt to use his one talent was accused of being wicked and lazy.

Whether we have just one talent, or are good at lots of things, what matters most is that we use our talents to the full in the service of others and in our service for God.

Optional conclusion

Listen to the words of this children's hymn:

>God entrusts to all
>Talents few or many
>None so young or small
>That they haven't any.
>
>God will surely ask
>'Ere I enter Heaven
>Have I done the task
>Which to me was given?

Prayer   No 3 and/or 4
Hymns   'Lord of all hopefulness'
    'Come my brothers, praise the Lord'

Year 1, Spring Term 33

A round tuit

WEEK 6

Aim   To illustrate the folly of procrastination
Visual aid   A 'round tuit' – either a plate or a cardboard replica (see below)

When I first saw one of these in a gift shop I wondered what on earth it was. Then I read the inscription on it and realised that it was what I had always needed. (*Read inscription.*)

    How often have you said to your teacher: 'I haven't done my homework because I didn't get around to it'? Or, to your Mum: 'I didn't tidy my bedroom because I didn't get around to it'?
    If I don't get around to doing a job and keep putting it off – it *never* seems to get done.
    There is a big word to describe this. It is 'procrastination'. Procrastination means putting off until tomorrow what you should do today. There is a saying, 'Procrastination is the thief of time'. What do you think it means?

Christian application

Most people have this experience. Even Jesus was aware of the danger of procrastination. He said, 'I must work the works of Him that sent me while it is day. The night cometh when no man can work.'

When someone asked Jesus for help he responded straight away.

Reading   John 9. 1–7
          We should always be ready to help others, rather than putting things off.
Prayer   No 13
Hymn   'Who would true valour see'
          'Go tell it on the mountain'

Doors

WEEK 7

Aim   To show that Jesus is "the way"
Visual aid (Optional)   A print of 'The Light of the World' by William Holman Hunt

I want us to think today about doors and how much they feature in our lives. How often, during the course of the day, do we open, close or pass through a door? Dozens of times, at least!

There are many different types of door:

    Front doors
    Back doors
    Cupboard doors
    Classroom doors
    Swing doors
    Sliding doors
    Revolving doors
    Trap doors
    Doors that won't open
    Doors that won't stay shut
    Can you think of any other examples?

    Let me tell you about a famous scientist who had two special doors made. Isaac Newton was fond of cats but when he was busy working in his study he was sometimes irritated by the scratching at his door and the 'meows' from his cat and her baby kitten who wanted to get in. At last he hit on a solution. He called in the carpenter and had two special doors made which the cats could open themselves. One door was larger than the other and was for the fully-grown mother cat. The other was much smaller and was for the baby kitten to use.

    What a stupid thing for a very clever person to do! Can you think why? Both the kitten and the cat could use the larger door. There was no need to have two doors made.

    All this has been by way of introduction for I really want to tell you of a most important and wonderful door.

Reading   John 10, 1–10.

         Jesus said, 'I am the DOOR to the Heavenly Kingdom.'
         He also said, 'I am the way, the truth and the life.' If we follow Jesus, we will be able to enter God's kingdom.

Optional conclusion

William Holman Hunt, a very famous artist, painted a picture called 'The Light of the World' (*Show reproduction*). It depicts Christ standing outside a door which is overgrown with weeds. There is no latch on the door. The door represents the door to a person's life. Jesus is knocking at that door, wanting to come in to help and to strengthen and to guide. The reason why there is no apparent latch is that the handle is on the inside!

Prayer   No 21
Hymn   'Thou didst leave thy home and thy kingly crown'
         'Seek ye first the kingdom of God'

Castles

WEEK 8

Aim   To encourage respect for other people's property
Visual aid   A picture of a castle

The theme of our assembly this morning is castles. I expect you've all visited a castle. There is always something exciting to do or see. Maybe you enjoy exploring the ramparts, the towers or the dungeons. You probably imagine the knights of old who lived in the castles and fought there to defend their territory. What castles have *you* visited?

People built castles for defence and protection. Many of these old strongholds are now in ruins, relics of a time when fierce battles were fought between different clans or kingdoms.

There is a saying that 'An Englishman's home is his castle'. This means that our homes are our own private possessions and that in our homes we should feel safe. Others should respect our privacy. But this saying does not seem to be as true today as it once was. It is very sad that we often hear of property being damaged or vandalised, of homes being broken into, and of treasured possessions being stolen by thieves.

Our homes should be our castles.

We must, for our part, respect other people's property.

Christian application

Theft and burglary were a problem in Jesus' time, as they are today. But Jesus told his followers about a different sort of treasure, which thieves could not steal.

Reading   Matthew 6, 19–21
            We can lay up 'treasure' in heaven by serving God and doing His will. This sort of treasure cannot be destroyed or stolen.
Prayer   No 12
Hymn   'When a knight won his spurs'

No answer? WEEK 9

Aim   To illustrate the extent of God's love for us
Visual aids   List of questions, as below. Invite 14 volunteers to read them out

One of the best ways of learning as we grow older is to ask questions and to try to find out the answers.

Some questions are very difficult to answer. Some questions cannot be answered at all. We sometimes say:

'There's no answer to that!'

Here are some questions which little children have asked, to which there seems to be no answer.

1. Now that we've got a new television will we get better programmes?
2. How can I find the word in the dictionary if I can't even spell it?
3. Mum, if you were Queen would you be Lily the First?
4. If I can't have more pocket money, can I have the same amount more often?
5. Why do teachers get paid when we do all the work?
6. Why didn't God make straight rivers?
7. How do pigs lay bacon?
8. Do sausages grow or are they born?
9. Why don't they make mouse-flavoured cat food?
10. If there are rainbows why aren't there snowbows?
11. How do fishes sit down?
12. Why do babies sleep all day and cry all night?
13. When God made the world what did he stand on?
14. Mum, why do I keep on asking questions?

But you must all keep on asking questions. It is the best way to learn. Never be afraid to ask questions when you don't understand.

We all laughed at the children's questions. But there are other, more serious questions which seem to have no answer: 'Why is there so much suffering in the world?', 'Why did my Granny have to die?', 'Why are there wars?', 'Why do innocent people suffer when there are disasters?'.

We cannot supply easy answers to these questions. All we can do is try to help anyone who is suffering or sad.

Christian application

The Bible gives the answers to some difficult questions, for example:

Qu: Who made the world?
Ans: 'In the beginning God created the Heaven and the earth.'
(*see Genesis 1, 1*)
Qu: How should we behave towards our fellow men?
Ans: 'We should love our neighbour as much as we love ourselves.'
(*see Luke 10, 27b*)
Qu: How much should we love God?
Ans: 'Love the Lord your God with all your heart, with all your mind, with all your soul and with all your strength.'
(*see Luke 10, 27a*)

'How much does God love us?' is a hard question to answer. We can't measure God's love to us. We can't put a price on God's love and say it is worth – so much. The Bible does tell us, however, that God loved us so much that He sent his son Jesus into the world to be our Saviour.

Reading John 3, 16
Prayer No 4
Hymn 'It is a thing most wonderful'
'God my Father loving me'
'He's got the whole world in His hand'

Bill stickers

WEEK 10

Aim To further explain the meaning of Easter
Visual aid Poster with the words:

Bill Stickers will be prosecuted

This morning's story is about a boy with a very funny name. His name was Bill and his surname was Stickers.

Bill Stickers, like most boys of his age, had a passion for jam tarts and it was this craving which got him into trouble. It would have been fine if his mother had not called him in to tell him she was just going to town. 'I've made some strawberry jam tarts and put them on the table in the kitchen to cool,' she said. 'See that you don't touch them. Be good!'

Now, if Bill's mother hadn't told him, he wouldn't have known the jam tarts were there, but now he knew and the temptation proved to be too great. 'Surely she won't miss one!' he thought.

He soon discovered that it was a very good jam tart indeed. So he took another. This seemed to be even better than the first. He couldn't resist a third, and a fourth and . . . By the time he had eaten seven he began to remember what his mother had said. He realised that she would soon notice that there were lots of jam tarts missing.

That was where he made his next mistake. He decided to run away. I suppose he thought his mother would be very cross. By now, Bill had a very guilty conscience. As he hurried down the road he met Mrs Brown, his mother's friend. Bill wiped his mouth because he felt sure Mrs Brown would guess that he had been stealing jam tarts. She would be able to see the jam on his face! Bill breathed a sigh of relief when Mrs Brown didn't notice and just said, 'Hello Bill!'

Shortly after this Bill received another shock, for who should be cycling down the road but the local police constable. Bill went very red in the face, with guilt, and when the policeman stopped, got off his bike and walked towards him, Bill thought he was going to say, 'Bill Stickers I have a warrant for your arrest for stealing your Mum's jam tarts.' What a relief when the policeman just walked past him and knocked on the door of a nearby house. But worse was to come. As he approached an empty shop in the high street, Bill saw this notice. (*Show poster: Bill Stickers will be prosecuted.*) Bill was horrified. He thought he had been found out! He didn't realise that the owner of the shop had put up the notice to prevent other people from sticking bills or advertisements on his wall.

Bill's conscience was telling him very firmly that he had done wrong. So now he began to put matters right. He turned round and ran home. His mother was waiting for him anxiously. Bill told her how sorry he was, that he had learnt his lesson and promised not to do it again.

It's a good job we all have a conscience – the little voice inside that tells us when we are doing wrong. If we always obeyed our consciences we would do very well. Sadly, we all sometimes do things we are ashamed of. Then we must apologise and try to put things right.

Christian application

We know that no matter what we do wrong, God will forgive us if we are truly sorry. This is why He sent His son Jesus into the world. A well-known Easter hymn says:

> '*He died that we might be forgiven*
> *He died to make us good.*'

Reading   First Epistle of John 1, 5–10
Prayer   No 20 (or 13)
Hymn   'There is a green hill far away'
            'Lord Jesus Christ, you have come to us'

Crooked sixpence WEEK 11

Aim   To get one's priorities 'straightened out'
Visual aid   An old sixpence

Can you see what this is? It is obviously a coin. It is a sixpence, a coin which is no longer legal tender. It is worth about two and a half pence in decimal currency. Listen to this poem about a sixpence.

> There was a crooked man
> Who walked a crooked mile
> He found a crooked sixpence
> Beside a crooked stile.
> He bought a crooked cat
> Which caught a crooked mouse
> And they all lived together
> In a little crooked house.

Everything in the poem is crooked. When things go wrong, it's easy to get disheartened and feel that the whole world is crooked. This is not true. There are some very beautiful things in the world and some very good, kind people.

But some people are wicked, so crooked in fact that they are described as 'crooks'.

Of course, we are not crooks. But at times we all do little things that are wrong. It is then that our lives become a little twisted. We need to get our lives and our priorities straightened out. Who is there to help us do this? Many people can help. Our parents, teachers, friends all help us to do the right thing and to 'go straight'.

Christian application

Jesus is best able to help us to lead straight-forward, good, honest, respectable lives. If we follow his teachings, we can play our part in helping to make the world a better place in which to live.

Reading   Galatians 5, 22–26
Prayer   No 14
Hymn   'Father lead me day by day'
           'Father I place into your hands'

Twice my own! WEEK 12

Aim To further illustrate God's forgiveness
Visual aid (optional) Model yacht

Like most boys of his age Timothy enjoyed making things. His latest project was a model yacht. With great care and patience he shaped the hull of the boat and then smoothed it down with glass paper. A mast and a boom were made out of lengths of dowel rod and he fitted these to the hull. He even sewed the sails himself out of some white material his mother provided. Finally he gave the boat several coats of bright red paint. It was finished in time for him to take on his holiday to the seaside. What a sense of satisfaction he derived from a job well done.

The great day arrived. Timothy went down to the rocky shore to see if his boat would sail. Success! the wind caught the sails and the boat cut speedily through the water.

Timothy's delight was short-lived, however, for a huge wave broke over the rocks and as it went out again it took with it Timothy's boat. He could only stand and stare as his boat was taken out to sea. Very sadly he walked away, thinking that that would be the last he would see of his boat.

What an unexpected happy ending there was to the story. The local church was holding a jumble sale the following day and it so happened that one of the church members, exercising his dog that morning, had found, washed up by the tide, a red model yacht. 'What a pity, some child has left this on the beach. There is no way I can possibly find the owner. I might as well try to get 50p for it at our jumble sale this afternoon.'

Timothy happened to glance in at the sale. Imagine his astonishment when he saw his own boat for sale. He didn't even try to explain that it was *his* boat; he eagerly handed in 50p to purchase it. As he left the church hall, clutching the red yacht, a lady helper heard him say to himself, 'Now it's twice my own, I made it and now I have bought it.'

This is what the Bible tells us God did at Easter time. He made us in the first place but He also bought us.

The book of Genesis teaches that God created the universe and He also created man in His own image. When men and women became cruel and disobedient this made God very sad. So He sent His Son into the world to teach us that God loves and cares and forgives. Jesus proved this by his death upon the cross. Though we may sometimes stray from God's ways, He has 'bought' us back again. The price He has paid is the gift of His Son. Christian people believe that this is why Jesus died upon the cross. Because we had strayed from God's ways; Jesus died to bring us back again.

(For background research see: I Peter 3, 13–18; I Peter 1, 1–19; John 12, 27; John 18, 37.)

Readings   John 3, 16–19
            and/or
            Isaiah 53, 1–6 (or the whole chapter)
Prayer   No 2
Hymns   'When I survey the wondrous cross'
            'In the cross of Christ I glory'
            'There is a green hill far away'

April fool!

WEEK 13

Aim To discourage foolish behaviour

'Please Sir! Your shoe lace is undone!'

Really this is such a well-known April Fool trick that you are not likely to catch anyone out with it. You will have to be more original. (*As an alternative introduction the presenter could play a joke on the pupils by, say, announcing a hymn, the number of which is not in the book. The decision rests on whether the children would respond suitably to this.*)

One of the best April Fool's tricks I can remember was played by the BBC some years ago. They reported on the spaghetti harvest and showed the crop growing on the trees and being gathered in. Many viewers were taken in by it and said, 'Well! I never knew that spaghetti grew on trees.' It was of course, a huge April Fool joke, for spaghetti is made from wheat.

No-one likes to realise that he has been made a fool of. It isn't good sportsmanship to make fun of the person who comes last in a race or who doesn't do well in a test. There should be no cause for such a person to feel foolish, providing they have tried their best.

Sometimes we have to admit that we have been foolish because our energies have been misdirected. Maybe we did not pay attention to the instructions given by our teacher and then we did the wrong piece of work. Perhaps we didn't listen carefully to what our mother or father asked us to get from the shops and we finished up bringing the wrong things. It is at times like these that we sometimes say to ourselves, 'I am a fool!'

Occasionally older boys and girls who have left school come back and say 'I wish I had my time to go over again. I would have worked much harder. When I was at school I spent too much time fooling about'. I hope you will never have cause to think that. Don't make a fool of yourself!

Christian application

Jesus once told a story about a man who behaved in a very foolish way.

Reading Luke 12, 16–21

How foolish we are if we attach more importance to worldly possessions than we attach to our service for God and our faith in Him. Indeed the Bible says that people who do not believe in God are fools. (See Psalm 14, 1.)

Prayer No 18

Hymn 'O Jesus I have promised' (modern tune)

Good news

WEEK 1

Theme The message of Easter
Visual aid A box of chocolates

I have good news for you this morning.
What has just flashed through your mind? Did you think

'Perhaps we are to have an extra day's holiday?'
or 'Maybe we're not going to have exams after all?'

If you were told to expect Good News what would you think of? (*Invite suggestions*.) Perhaps one of the following:

- a relative or friend who you haven't seen for years is going to visit you?
- an aunt has invited you to stay with her for a holiday?
- a rich uncle has sent you a hundred pounds?
- your parents have bought you a new bicycle?
- you have just been told that you have been selected to play for the school team?
- you have just come top of the class in an exam?
- you might even think that I have bought you a box of chocolates bearing the name – Good News!

All these would indeed be good news but not the best news. Let me tell you about the best news of all.

Reading (Matthew 28, 1–8 – the Resurrection story (use the Good News Bible if possible)
        The reading was from Matthew's gospel. The word 'gospel' itself means good news and the reading was from the Good News Bible. The good news is that Jesus rose from the dead and is alive today. Christian people believe that the Spirit of Jesus is at work in the world today, working in and through the lives of all those people who are His followers.
Prayer No 23
Hymns 'Jesus Christ is risen today'
       'Morning has broken, like the first morning'
       'Lord of the dance'

Cricket

Theme   Keeping the rules
Visual aid Tea towel or apron with the 'rules for cricket' (these may be obtained from many gift shops). Alternatively, the rules could be displayed on a board, or simply read aloud

As the cricket season is about to start and since cricket is our national sport I thought it would be appropriate if I explained the rules of the game. I have a copy here.

The Rules of Cricket
(as explained to a foreign visitor)

You have two sides, one out in the field and one in.

Each man that's in the side that's in goes out and when he's out he comes in and the next man goes out until he's out.

When they are all out the side that's out comes in and the side that's been in goes out and tries to get those coming in out.

When both sides have been in and out including the not outs that's the end of the game!

These rules seem very complicated and very confusing. It is a good job that our school rules aren't as difficult to understand. (*Give examples of school rules, or ask pupils to suggest some.*) Think for a moment about how important our school rules are, for example: 'No running inside the building'. This is a very sensible rule: if everyone ran about, there would often be collisions and accidents. All our rules are really matters of common sense – and they are for our own benefit.

Christian application

Now let us see how clear and precise God's rules are.

Reading   Luke 10, 25–37
          These rules can be summed up as 'Love God and love your neighbour'. But although these rules are very easy to understand, most people find them very difficult to keep. We need to ask God to help us keep His rules.
Prayer   No 17
Hymns   'Heavenly Father may Thy blessing'
          'O Lord all the world belongs to you'

Hallmarks

WEEK 3

Theme   Encouraging good behaviour – setting an example
Visual aids   Bradbury's *Book of Hallmarks* (or similar)
              Watchmaker's eye glass

I don't suppose many of you are interested in antiques but you may well have some very old articles at home and wonder if they are made of real gold or silver.

To find out, you should first look carefully to see if the item has a hallmark. This is a very tiny mark, stamp or picture stamped in an inconspicuous place on the metal. It may show a coat of arms, a lion's head, a castle or a monarch's head. To see it clearly you will need a watchmaker's eye glass or a powerful magnifying glass.

If you *do* find a hallmark, a guide such as Bradbury's Book of Hallmarks helps you ascertain the quality of the silver or gold; you will also be able to tell who made it, where it was made and the year it was made. This will give you a good idea as to its true value.

A hallmark, then, on an item such as a gold chain, a piece of silver jewellery or a sports trophy will tell you if the item is genuine and indicate whether it is valuable.

People have hallmarks too, though not marks that you can actually see on our bodies. Our lives and the way we live are our hallmarks.

These are some of the hallmarks I would like to see on pupils of this school:

    Smart appearance
    Courtesy
    Obedience
    Honesty
    Service
    Reliability
    Helpfulness
    Kindliness
    Appreciativeness
    Friendliness
    Generosity . . .

Christian application

Reading Ephesians 6. 13–18
   Can people see from our actions that we are followers of Jesus Christ?
Prayer No 12
Hymn 'When a Knight won his spurs'

At sixes and sevens WEEK 4

Aim To encourage good order

'I'm not at all satisfied with your work. You are all at sixes and sevens.'

When a teacher makes such a statement you will gather that your work has been very disorderly and confused. The phrase 'at sixes and sevens' is often used in such situations – but how did it originate?

One possible explanation dates back to the fourteenth century and the days of the old Livery Companies or Craft Guilds. From time to time these Guilds would hold a ceremonial procession through the streets of London. The oldest company would lead the procession with the rest following in order of seniority. On one such occasion a quarrel broke out between the Merchant Taylors and a Guild called Skinners. They could not agree who should be sixth and who seventh in the procession. They were all at sixes and sevens and began to fight . . .

Eventually the two Guilds came to an agreement, helped by the Lord Mayor of London. The solution was obvious. They would take it in turns. One year one group would take sixth position and the following year the seventh place. They also agreed to entertain each other on alternate years to a banquet.

There is an interesting story in the Old Testament as to how the many different and confusing languages in the world today came about. (Read the story of the Tower of Babel: Genesis 11, 1–9).

What utter confusion there must have been! These people were really at sixes and sevens. Their trouble was that they had become full of their own importance. They had even begun to build a huge tower by which they intended climbing up to heaven. But their efforts met with disaster and they became thoroughly disorganised.

The lesson we must learn is that *everyone* suffers when we are at sixes and sevens. Our school sports teams would never win a match if each member played as an individual, with no thought for others in the team. Sporting success depends on the members of a team relying and thinking about each other, and playing together as a team.

A school is a much happier place when every member tries to be helpful and shows concern and respect for others.

Christian application

A good motto for our lives comes from Psalm 71 (verse 1):
'In Thee, O Lord, do I put my trust, let me never be put to confusion.'

Prayer No 6 or 19
Hymns 'All things bright and beautiful' (a hymn which speaks of the orderliness of God's creation)
'Let us with a gladsome mind'

Sailing

WEEK 5

Aim   To explain the significance of Whitsuntide
Visual aid A burgee (ie a small triangular flag on a rod, approximately half a metre long)
Reading   Acts 2. 1–4

The reading was an account of the events of the first Whit Sunday, the day when the disciples of Jesus first received the power of His Spirit in their lives. What a change came over them all. They had previously been too scared to venture outside in case they were arrested and killed like Jesus. The disciples had remained hidden away in an upper room.

But now they felt the power of the Holy Spirit and the change was immediate. Out into the streets and market places they went, boldly preaching the good news about Jesus.

It is very difficult to understand what is meant by the Holy Spirit so here is a little illustration which I hope will help.

You will all immediately recognise this as a flag.

It is, however, a special sort of flag called a burgee. If you have ever seen sailing boats you may have noticed that they all have one of these burgees at the top of the mast.

The flag is not there for decoration or even to show which sailing club the boat belongs to. Its purpose is far more important. Burgees tell the helmsman (the person steering the boat) the direction in which the wind is blowing. This information is vital, for the helmsman has then to set the sails and steer the best course according to the direction of the wind.

Have you ever seen wind? No. But you have seen the effects of the wind: blowing the flag on the top of the mast; blowing the leaves off trees; blowing sand on a windswept beach.

This is similar to the work of the Holy Spirit. We can't see the Holy Spirit but we know that it is God's power and strength and we can see the effects of this power in people's lives.

Jesus said, 'The wind blows where it wills. You can hear the sound of it but you cannot actually see it. This is so with the Spirit.' God promises to give His Spirit (ie His power and help) to all who ask for it.

Prayer   No 20
Hymn   'Holy, holy, holy, Lord God Almighty' (modern tune)
           'Father we love you'

Cold shoulder

WEEK 6

Theme Kindness and consideration

'Please Miss, I used to have Sarah Jones as my best friend but now she has started to be friendly with Tracy Brown and she won't speak to me. Whenever I try to be friendly she turns away and gives me the cold shoulder.'

'Please Sir, none of the boys in the class will speak to me. It is ever since Steven Williams said I had taken his pencil case and I've never touched it. But all the class now give me the cold shoulder.'

Now that phrase 'to give someone the cold shoulder' has an interesting origin.

The cold shoulder refers to a shoulder of lamb. In the nineteenth century if you arranged a dinner party and invited several guests they would expect to be given several different courses including a main course with hot meat such as roast beef or roast lamb. If one of the guests had behaved in a way which displeased the host or had said something to cause offence he would be served with a dish of, say, cold mutton or a cold shoulder of lamb. This was the host's way of giving the offending guest a broad hint that he was out of favour and no longer welcome in his circle of friends. He had been given the cold shoulder.

How much better it would be if, instead of giving someone the cold shoulder, we tried to understand their point of view and settled our differences.

Christian application

In the teaching of Jesus there is no room for 'giving the cold shoulder' to anyone. In fact Jesus teaches quite the reverse:

Reading   Luke 6, 31–38
           How much better the world would be if people tried to live according to this teaching.
Prayer   No 19
Hymns   'God make my life a little light'
          'Looking upward every day'
          'Give me oil in my lamp'

Sand experiment

WEEK 7

Aim   To give an awareness of the magnitude of God's creation
Visual aids   Some dry sand, a thimble, a bucket and a torch.

Preparation

Prior to the assembly arrange for a group of 32 pupils to conduct an experiment. Pour one thimbleful of sand on to a sheet of paper. Divide the sand as equally as possible into two small piles. Then divide these again into 4, 8, 16 and finally 32 approximately equal piles.

Now ask each pupil to count the number of grains of sand in a pile!

Add the 32 numbers together (use a calculator!) to find the number of grains of sand in a thimble. The number, of course, will be very approximate, but will suffice.

Assembly

This morning we are going to conduct an experiment with sand. How many grains do you think are contained in this thimble? It is full. Count them quietly to yourself as I pour them on to this sheet of paper.

There are 18 623 gains of sand here (or whatever number you came up with). I must confess that I had some help and would like to thank the members of Form . . . . . for counting the grains for me before the assembly.

Now, how many thimbles do you think it would take to fill this bucket? We are not going to bother counting – but it would be a very great number. Try now to imagine how many grains there would be in a bucketful! Next, try to imagine how many buckets of sand you could get from the beach at Bournemouth and Eastbourne and Hastings and Scarborough and Southport and Blackpool . . .

How many buckets of sand could you get from all the beaches in the entire country? The entire world . . .? Then try, if you can, to imagine how many thimbles of sand you could get from all the beaches in the entire world! The number is too vast for our minds to comprehend.

Now multiply this by 18 623 and you have got the number of grains of sand in the world.

Why have we conducted this experiment? I'll tell you later.

Before I do I want to talk to you about stars, those tiny stars which fill the night sky. As little children you may have sung 'Twinkle, twinkle little star'. You could not have been more wrong. In comparison with the stars our own earth is very much smaller.

The stars only look tiny because they are so far away – so far that we do not measure the distance in miles, but in what we call light years. Now this needs a little word of explanation. When I switch on this torch, the beam seems to reach the far wall almost instantaneously, but in fact it does take a tiny fraction of a second to cross the room. This is called the speed of light. Obviously light travels a very long way in a whole year. This is called a light year. Perhaps you can now understand that the stars are so far away that they are hundreds, thousands, even millions of light years away.

If your minds can take any more, here is the most amazing fact. Astronomers have said that there are probably as many stars, not just in the universe but in outer space as well, as there are grains of sand in the world. Each star, each planet has its own orbit. What an amazing universe we live in.

Christian application

This is how the Bible begins the story of the creation:

> 'In the beginning God created the heavens and the earth.' (Genesis 1, 1.)

When we think of the vastness of God's creation we seem no more important than tiny grains of sand. But this is not so, for we are told that God is a loving Father who is concerned about every detail of our lives. Jesus said that even the hairs of our head are numbered (Matthew 10, 30).

Reading   Psalm 8
Prayer   No 26
Hymns   'For the beauty of the earth'
            'Who put the colours in the rainbow?'

Trivial pursuit

WEEK 8

Theme   Getting on with the job. Putting first things first
Visual aid   Game of *Trivial Pursuit*

I expect some of you recognise this game. *Trivial Pursuit* is a light-hearted and yet educational game which has become very popular in recent years. It is a very pleasant way of spending an evening with friends or relations. Some of the questions seem very easy – some are quite difficult. For example:

Qu: 'Where does the Trans-Siberian Railway start and finish?'
Ans: Moscow to Vladivostok.

Qu: 'What has 336 pimples?'
Ans: A golf ball.

Qu: 'How many Russians have set foot on the moon?'
Ans: None.

The name is indeed appropriate – "Trivial Pursuit".
When you really think about it, there is nothing trivial about gaining knowledge and becoming educated. This is a matter which should be taken very seriously. There should be nothing trivial about our work at school. It lays the foundations for the rest of our lives.

Christian application

Listen to what the Bible says about the reward we get for seeking wisdom:

Reading Proverbs 2, 1–10
Prayer   No 18
Hymns   'Fight the good fight'
           'God is love – sing aloud'

Rust

WEEK 9

Aim   To guard against temptation
Visual aid   Any rusty object

Do you know of anyone who is getting a new car? Perhaps you have heard them say 'My car is falling to pieces, it has become a rusty old heap, there is only one thing for it – I shall have to get a new one.'

Cars are made of steel. Steel is a *ferrous* metal – that is, it contains iron. Though this makes the metal very strong it also causes it to rust – especially if the car is left outside in the rain and damp. You may have studied the causes of rust in your science or DT lessons.

At first the rust may be a tiny spot, just a blemish in the paintwork. But the wise motorist tackles the rust straight away, before it grows any bigger. Otherwise it will spread and corrode the metal until it falls into holes.

Temptations are a bit like rust. The more we give way to the temptation to do wrong, the worse it gets. The 'rust' in our lives is the unkind and hurtful things we do, our selfish thoughts – all the things that spoil our lives and the lives of other people. We should guard against such things, just as the motorist guards against rust.

Christian application

Listen to what Jesus said about rust:

Reading   Matthew 6, 19–21
Prayer   No 2
Hymn   'The King of love my Shepherd is'

Up to scratch

WEEK 10

Aim To help assess performance in examinations

Did you know that many of the expressions we use in everyday conversation are taken from boxing? Here are some examples:

> to hit below the belt
> saved by the bell
> to pull one's punches
> to take it on the chin
> to throw in the towel

In the early days of boxing a mark or line was scratched in the middle of the boxing ring. According to the rules a boxer would lose the bout if, after being knocked down, he was still too groggy to walk unsupported to the scratch within an official period of 38 seconds. If he was not able to 'come up to scratch' he was considered unfit to continue the match and his opponent was declared the winner.

The term 'coming up to scratch' is no longer just associated with boxing. It is used whenever standards are set which we have to maintain. When you take an examination you hope that you will come up to scratch. If you reach the required pass-mark you will be up to scratch. If you know that you have done as well as you possibly can then as far as you are concerned you can feel well satisfied, for your year's work will be up to scratch. We can't all come first but we do all come up to scratch if we can say with a clear conscience, "I know I have done my best." If we feel we could have done better we should resolve that next term we will try to come up to scratch.

Christian application

God also requires that we should come up to scratch, but his standards are very high. He says, 'Be ye perfect as your Heavenly Father is perfect'.

Reading Romans 12, 1–3

In fact, these standards are so high that we cannot possibly hope to reach them without help. In Romans 3, 23, Saint Paul makes it clear that we all fall short of God's standards. None of us comes up to scratch. If we try to do things by our own

efforts we always fall short of the mark, but through God's grace, received as a free gift, we can continue to try to improve our lives.
Prayer   No 3
Hymn   'Jesus good above all other'

Sport

WEEK 11

Aim   To encourage singlemindedness
Visual aids   Three cards with the words 'boxing', 'athletics' and 'fishing'

In this season when sporting activities reach their climax I thought it would be appropriate if we considered three 'sports' mentioned in the Bible.

1. The first is boxing – or, at least, fighting. Fighting may seem very contradictory to the teaching of Jesus. He said that we should love our enemies. But the fight we are engaged in is the battle against the evil in the world, for example poverty, hunger, jealousy, envy, bitterness, hatred. These are things we must fight against.
   In the Bible this is called the 'good fight of the faith'. I hope we will one day be able to say, like Paul, 'I have fought the good fight, I have kept the faith.' (*See II Timothy, 4, 7*).
2. In what ways should we be like athletes? (*See I Corinthians 9, 25; Hebrews 12, 1*). Paul, in his first letter to the Church at Corinth says that we should learn to exercise self-control, just like a good athlete. The writer of the letter to the Hebrews tells us that we are like people running in a race and as such we should be patient.
3. Lastly, Jesus wants us to take up fishing. He said to two of his disciples, 'Follow me and I will make you fishers of men.' By the way we live our lives and by what we say to other people we should encourage them to live as Jesus wants them to live and become his followers too. In this way we become fishers of men.

Christian application

In any sporting competition there can be only one winner for there is usually only one prize. If we are faithful to God we are *all* promised the best prize of all, a place in God's heavenly kingdom.

Reading   Hebrews 12, 1–3
Prayer   No 16
Hymns   'Fight the good fight'
           'Onward Christian Soldiers'
           'Be bold, be strong'

Cheque books

WEEK 12

Theme   Just rewards
Visual aids A cheque book and a paying-in book

Do you belong to a savings bank? Saving a small sum regularly while you are young is a very good habit to get into. When you are older you will have one of these (*show paying-in book*) and one of these (*show cheque book*). Anyone can pay money into another person's account, providing they have the person's account number. But they can't draw money out of it. Only you can draw money out of your own account and you have to sign the cheque yourself in order to do so. This is a safeguard to prevent others drawing money out of your account.

If I put £10 into my account I can then draw out £10 when I need the money. If I put £100 into my account I will be able to draw out up to £100. I can't draw out more than I put in. When people try to draw out more than they put in it causes many problems.

You all have another sort of bank account. The bank is your mind. Here, too, you can only draw out what you put in.

The boy or girl who only reads comics will never be able to quote Shakespeare.

The pupil who does not work hard at school will not be able to answer questions when exams come round.

When we train hard, revise hard and work hard at our lessons we are paying in to our life's bank account. Later on, we will be able to draw out from this bank account at the appropriate time.

Look back over the past school year. How much have we put into our account? We can only expect to draw out, when necessary, what we have put in.

Christian application

Readings II Corinthians 9, 6–10
            Philippians 4, 4–8
Prayers   No 9 and 7
Hymn   'Praise to the Lord, the Almighty'
            'One more step'

Year 2

Fred WEEK 1

Theme Welcome to new school and/or year group

This morning I am going to tell you about Fred. Fred lived for 12 years, which is quite a good age for a goldfish! Fred's owner won him at a fairground, and he was brought home in a plastic bag full of water. On arrival he was transferred to the goldfish bowl where he lived contentedly, on his own, for about eight years. At first he was less than two inches long but by the time he was eight years old he had grown to be about six inches long, almost too big for the goldfish bowl.

Then, one day, something exciting happened. Fred's owner moved to a new house with a large garden and a goldfish pond in which there were already several goldfish. As Fred was too large now for his goldfish bowl he was transferred to the much larger garden pond.

At first he remained still, on the bottom of the pond, not knowing where to go but after a while be began to find his way around and within a day or two he was swimming merrily with the other fish, exploring the pond and getting used to his new suroundings.

In life we sometimes have a similar experience. When we move to new surroundings it sometimes takes a little time to settle in. At first things seem very strange. It is like this for you as you move from junior school to secondary school. You may have been used to being like a large fish in a small bowl. Perhaps you had important jobs to do, helping to organise the school and looking after younger children. Now you discover that everyone is older than you. You have become once again a small fish in a large pond.

Don't think, however, that you are not important. We all have our part to play in the smooth running of the school. It will not take long before you feel 'at home' and part of your new year group with new friends and exciting things to do.

Christian application

Just as we are all important to the life of our new school, so we are important in God's sight too. We should never feel insignificant or unimportant for God knows all about us and cares for each one of us. This reading tells us how much God cares.

Reading Matthew 6, 25–34
Prayer No 36
Hymn 'Let us with a gladsome mind'
         'One more step'

Flags 1   WEEK 2

Theme   To show the value of help and good advice
Visual aids   Pictures of various flags as illustrated on page 67
Note   The theme is suitable for presentation at a festival service or form assembly. Pupils may be rehearsed to read or recite the various parts. For a shorter assembly the presenter should be selective. Alternatively the theme could be spread over several assemblies.

Before the days of morse code, radio and radar, ships used flags for sending messsages to each other. They are still used today as a back-up for other means of communication at sea. Each different flag has its own special meaning, not just simply to denote what nationality the ship is or to which company it belongs. We can learn some lessons from these.

When any ship is about to sail on a great voyage this flag is hoisted (*1*). It is called the Blue Peter. The popular TV programme *Blue Peter* is appropriately called by that name because it is a programme for young people who have just started out on a great journey through life. You have just begun your career at your new school.

Once a ship is on the high seas it may encounter hazards of many different sorts – storms, icebergs, difficult currents, tides, hidden rocks or sand banks. Or something may go wrong with the ship itself, so that it is not able to continue its journey. Should this happen the captain will fly this flag (*2*). It means 'I am disabled'. We all sometimes have difficulties to overcome and hazards to face. We may be tempted to tell lies, to be disobedient or just to be lazy or unkind. All these things are like the hidden sand banks or rocks. They impede our journey through life.

When a ship gets into serious trouble – if, say, it is taking in water or its engines have failed – the crew hoist this flag (*3*). It means 'I need help'. In our lives we should never be too proud or stubborn to ask for help when we need it. We should always be prepared to accept good advice.

It is a captain's duty to point out to other vessels that they may be heading for danger. This flag (*4*) means 'You are in danger'.

We too have a duty to warn other people of danger so that they will not get into trouble.

This flag (*5*) means simply 'Yes'. A captain may fly this flag in answer to a question from a passing ship. There are times when we should fly an imaginary flag like this in answer to questions such as:

> 'Are you prepared to lend a helping hand?'
> 'Are you always kind and friendly?'
> 'Do you always work to the best of your ability?'

This one (6) means 'No'. Do you sometimes lose your temper? No? If someone does something to offend you, will you retaliate? No? If someone does something wrong and tries to persuade you to do the same, will you say No?

There are times when the coastguards may instruct a ship to 'Stop at once'. This is the message this flag (7) conveys. Maybe the guards suspect that the ship is being used for smuggling or carrying illegal immigrants. When we see others behaving in an irresponsible way it is our duty to tell them to stop at once. We should play our part in trying to put a stop to stealing, vandalism, mugging etc.

It is not difficult to say 'stop'. We ought to explain to people that there is a better way to behave which will make the world a happier place. This flag (8) says 'Stop, I wish to communicate with you.'

As a ship approaches a harbour a wise captain will fly this flag (9). It means 'Pilot wanted'. He is asking for a pilot, who knows all the dangerous currents, hidden rocks or treacherous sand banks, to come on board his ship to guide it safely into the harbour. Never be afraid to ask for help.

Christian application

Many of the flags could have a further significance for Christian people. For example:

5th Flag We should be able to answer Yes to the following questions.

- Do you say your prayers?
- Do you read the Bible?
- Do you wish to be a follower of the Lord Jesus?

6th Flag We should be able to answer No to the following questions.

- Do you behave in a way which lets Jesus down?
- Do you ever take the name of the Lord in vain?

8th Flag Christian people should try to communicate the Gospel to others and in this way seek to extend God's kingdom of love in the world.

9th Flag We too have a 'pilot'. Our Heavenly Father will be our guide throughout our lives, and Jesus Christ will be with us if we ask Him.

Once the pilot has come on board the ship this flag is hoisted (10). It indicates that there is a 'pilot on board'. The pilot then guides the ship

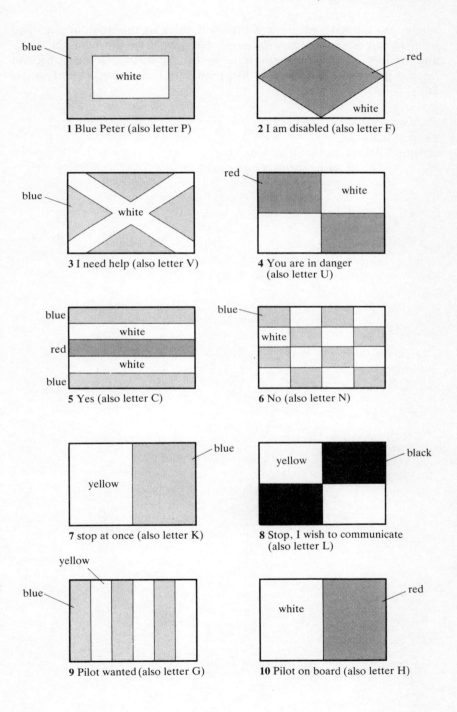

safely into the harbour. Jesus Christ will guide us through our lives and bring us safely to our Heavenly home. He says, 'I am the Way, the Truth and the Life – no man cometh to the Father but by me' (John 14, 6), and he also promises his followers, 'Lo, I am with you always' (Matthew 28, 20).

Reading   John 14, 1–6
Prayer   No 28
Hymn   'Now thank we all our God'
           'Lead us heavenly Father lead us'

Flags 2   WEEK 3

Theme   Doing our duty
Visual aids Flags used in previous demonstration

We have already considered some of the special meanings of different flags. In addition to this each flag stands for a letter of the alphabet.

So if the captain of a ship wishes to send a special message he may string lots of flags together to spell out the words.

One of the most famous messages displayed in this way was the one which Admiral Lord Nelson flew from his flagship at the Battle of Trafalgar. The message read as follows:

'England expects this day that every man should do his duty.'

This inspired the British sailors to achieve a glorious victory, although sadly Nelson himself died in the battle.

The message for us today is that our school expects this day that every boy and girl shall do their duty.

Christian application

We have a responsibility to live as God would have us live and to do only that which will help to better the life of our school.

Reading Psalm 100
Prayer   No 38
Hymn   'Forth in Thy name O Lord we go'
         'Go tell it on the mountain'

Ants

WEEK 4

Aim To encourage good order and industry.

You've probably often been told to be as quiet as mice. But never before will you have been told to be like ants!

In the Lake District one of the most magnificent views is from the top of a cliff overlooking Derwentwater. It is called 'Surprise View'. Thousands of visitors view the lake and the distant mountains each year but an equally wonderful sight goes unnoticed. If only they would look down at their feet they would see an amazing sight, for there, running along the top of the cliff for hundreds of yards is a narrow path, only six inches wide. It has been worn over many years by a vast colony of ants. On a fine day, if you are observant, you will see these ants, millions of them, all going about their business in an orderly manner. There are worker ants and soldier ants all moving to and fro with their special jobs to do. They collect bark, small pieces of straw and tiny twigs. The latter they use as 'ant-made' bridges to cross mini-ravines as they take plant seeds to their granaries which have been built in special chambers in the ants' nest.

We do well to take an example from the ants. We should busily set about the tasks we are given in our lessons, storing away all the information in our minds for future use. Success will not come our way if we waste our time. If we are wise and wish to succeed, then, like the ant, we must work industriously.

Christian application

King Solomon was well-known for his wisdom. He too must have realised how much we can learn from observing the behaviour of ants. This is what he wrote in the book of Proverbs:

Reading Proverbs 6, 6–11
Prayer   No 26
Hymn   'For the beauty of the earth'

What Tommy owes   WEEK 5

Harvest theme   How much we owe to God. Showing gratitude to others
Visual aids   Two 'accounts' (see below). Several items of harvest produce

Tommy was desperately in need of more pocket money. He sat thinking how he could earn more. Suddenly he had what he considered was a brilliant idea. He would present his mother with a bill for all the extra jobs he had been doing around the house.

The following morning Tommy's mother found a folded piece of paper on the breakfast table. She carefully unfolded it and this is what she read:

MOTHER OWES TOMMY

1	For keeping his bedroom tidy	40p
2	For running errands	40p
3	For doing his piano practice (which he hated)	80p
4	For washing his neck (which he hated)	80p
5	For being good (which he had been for most of the time)	60p
	TOTAL:	£3.00

Tommy's mother was obviously taken aback but said nothing. She simply placed three one pound coins by Tommy's plate on the breakfast table. When he came down he was delighted. His plan had worked. Now he would be able to buy the new toy he badly needed.

The following day, however, when Tommy came down for breakfast he, too, found a folded piece of paper on his plate. When he opened it he felt very sad indeed. It said:

TOMMY OWES MOTHER

1	For preparing all his meals	NOTHING
2	For doing all the housework	NOTHING
3	For taking him on holiday	NOTHING
4	For providing all his clothes	NOTHING
5	For nursing him when sick	NOTHING
	TOTAL:	NOTHING

Tommy realised that his mother always did these things, not for reward, but because she loved him. He learned a very important lesson that day and always remembered in future to show his appreciation for all that his parents did for him.

Christian application

We may fall into a similar 'trap' ourselves in taking God for granted and not thanking Him for all His goodness and His love.

Around us today we have the evidence of His love in providing so many good things for us. We remember at Harvest Time God's providence and His care for His children, and we are reminded that we must love God and that it is our duty to care for other people.

Reading Psalm 19, 1–10
Prayer   No 32
Hymn   'We plough the fields and scatter'
           'Come, ye thankful people, come'
           'God knows me'

Shoelaces WEEK 6

Aim To illustrate our dependence upon other people and upon God
Visual aid A pair of shoelaces

Simon's trouble was that he was always boasting. One day he boasted to the others in his form that he could pull himself up, off the ground, by tugging at his own shoelaces.

'Right,' they all said, 'give us a demonstration!'

Simon obligingly stooped down and took hold of his shoelaces. He pulled for all his worth but, of course, did not manage to pull himself up even a millimetre, from the floor. Simon didn't like being laughed at.

'You'll see,' he said, 'give me just one week and I'll get myself really fit, then I will show you.'

Simon spent the week weight training, toning up his muscles and generally trying to make himself fitter and stronger.

'Now I'll show you,' he announced and all his class-mates gathered round to watch. Simon heaved with all his might but to no avail. Howls of laughter greeted his second miserable failure.

'I know what the trouble is,' he said, 'I'm overweight. Give me a chance to lose a few pounds and then I really will prove that I can pull myself up by tugging at my own shoelaces.'

For a whole week Simon went on a diet. No sweets. No chocolate. No biscuits. No cream cakes. No fish and chips. He was determined that he would prove his point. When the time came for the final demonstration he had lost quite a few pounds and felt very confident.

This time he took a really good hold of his own shoelaces, with all the other members of the form standing round. He took one almighty tug at the shoelaces, and guess what happened? The shoelaces snapped!

'We told you so, we told you so! It isn't possible to pull yourself up by tugging at your own shoelaces!'

This story teaches us all a very important lesson. Of course, as we grow older we should try to become self-reliant. On the other hand, as we progress through school and later life we should never be too proud to accept help. Simon could only 'pick himself up' with the help of other people. There are lots of people ready to help you with your work and with any problems you may have at school or outside. Your friends, your teachers, your parents, youth leaders, church leaders – all are willing to help. Listen carefully to good advice and accept help whenever you find things too difficult.

Christian application

Some people feel that they can reach God's Kingdom entirely by their own efforts, but this is not what the Bible teaches (see Romans 3, 23). On our own we are simply not good enough. We all need God's help and His forgiveness (see 1 John 1, 8–9). This is given to us freely (Ephesians 2, 8–9).

Reading 1 John 1, 8–10
Prayer   No 37
Hymns   'Soldiers of Christ, arise'
           'When I needed a neighbour'

Horseshoe nail

WEEK 7

Aim To show that we each have an important part to play
Visual aid A horseshoe nail

If any of you are fortunate to have a horse or pony of your own, or if you have had riding lessons, you will probably recognise this object. It is a horseshoe nail. Great care and attention must be paid by owners to see that their horses are properly shod. Here is a poem about a Horseshoe Nail:

> For want of a nail the shoe was lost,
> For want of a shoe the horse was lost,
> For want of a horse the rider was lost,
> For want of a rider the message was lost,
> For want of a message the battle was lost,
> For want of a battle the kingdom was lost,
> And all for the want of a horseshoe nail.

Who would have thought that the loss of a tiny nail like this would have directly caused the downfall of a kingdom? Because the loss of the nail caused the horse to go lame, the rider was not able to get the warning message to the king's army in time to prevent a great disaster. Even a tiny nail was important.

We are all important in the life of our school. Careless work, careless talk, careless behaviour can seriously hamper the life of our school. We each have an important part to play and should never feel that we are too insignificant to matter.

Christian application

Similarly we are all important in God's sight. He knows all about us and cares for us. Even 'the very hairs of your head are all numbered'.

Reading Matthew 6, 25–34
Prayer No 15
Hymn 'O Jesus I have promised'
   'Bind us together, Lord'

Jigsaws — WEEK 8

Aim To demonstrate the importance of the individual
Visual aids Two jigsaws – one in a box with a picture and one without a picture

Do you like doing jigsaws? When doing a jigsaw it is a good idea to have a system. For example, you might first find the four corner pieces, then all the straight bits, and assemble them. Study the picture very closely and decide which part you are going to do first, eg sort out the 'brick' pieces for the walls of houses or sort out all the blue pieces for the sky or sea, etc.

It gives a great deal of satisfaction when the picture is eventually complete but how disappointing it is if you discover one or two pieces missing. The whole effect is spoiled.

How much more difficult it would be if your jigsaw is like this one. It has no picture to copy from. We do not even know what is the subject of the jigsaw.

What can we learn from jigsaws? First, every piece of a jigsaw is important and if one piece is missing the whole effect is spoiled. In the same way each member of the school is important and if just one person does not pull his/her weight or does not behave properly then the whole effect is ruined. The reputation of the school is damaged.

Second, we all need a picture to copy or an example to follow – like the picture on a jigsaw box. We should follow the good example of older pupils, older brothers, sisters and parents.

Christian application

The best example for us to try to copy is that of the Lord Jesus Christ, who when he was here upon earth had the same experiences that we have.

> 'For He is our childhood's pattern
> Day by day like us He grew'

Optional conclusion

Each piece of a jigsaw has its proper place, the pieces fitting perfectly together. It should be so with Christian people. They are all members of 'The body of Christ' today in the world, that is, the Christian Church (*See*

1 Corinthians 12, 12). Christian people all have a special part to play in fulfilling God's plans and purpose in the world. They should work harmoniously together.

Reading　Ephesians 4, 11–16 (A modern translation is recommended for this passage, eg Living Bible)
Prayer　No 12
Hymn　'Jesus good above all other'

It's a changing world   WEEK 9

Aim   To show that Jesus remains the same. To show that there are some values which should remain the same in every generation

> 'It wasn't like that when I was a lad!'
> 'Things are different these days!'
> 'Things aren't what they used to be!'
> 'The world is changing – and not always for the better!'

You must surely have heard older people making statements like these. You may agree that in some ways things have changed for the worst – but in many cases the changes have been for the better. For example, how many of your mothers get up at 7 am on Mondays to light the fire under the boiler in the wash-house and then, when the washing has been boiled, put it through the mangle and finally starch the shirt collars and dolly-blue the net curtains? Your mothers will agreed that, in this respect it is a good job the world has changed. Nowadays most people just put the washing into the automatic washing machine, switch it on and go out. When they return home later the washing is already done and dried.

Here is another example to show how the world has changed over the past hundred years. I'm going to read three short extracts from children's stories.

> 'Any girl with musical tendencies can learn sufficient in a few weeks to enable her to improve a piano which is very badly out of tune. What is not so easy, and only attainable by years of practice, is the ability to get absolute perfection of octaves and unisons.'

You probably didn't understand a word of what I have just read. No wonder! It was from the *Girls' Own Paper* of 1887.

Now listen to the beginning of a story from an annual for 1925.

> 'Once upon a time there lived a little Princess named Stella who had blue eyes and golden curls.'

Many stories in those days began with the words 'Once upon a time'.

Now our third example.

> 'Whoosh! Yowl! Kazam! Shplatt! Aagh! Grrr! Thwack! Eeeaarrgghh!.'

Yes you have guessed correctly – I have just read from an up-to-date comic strip cartoon! Perhaps I have been very unfair to modern writers but I have tried to show that even in children's literature times have changed over the past 100 years.

In a changing world we should always cherish those qualities which should never change: goodness, kindness, helpfulness, respect etc. It is encouraging that in every generation there are societies such as Dr Barnardos, NSPCC, Shelter which cater for people who need help. Their efforts to relieve suffering are unchanging.

Christian application

In so many ways our world is changing, and not always for the better. But in a changing world let us remember that there is someone who remains the same. That person is Jesus. In the Epistle to the Hebrews, 13, 8 we are told that:

> 'Jesus Christ is the same yesterday, today and for ever.'

Jesus loves people today just as he always did. Jesus will guide people today just as he always did. Jesus will help people and strengthen his followers today just as he always did. Jesus still remains the same.

Reading Hebrews 13, 5–8
Prayer No 1
Hymns 'God my Father loving me'
'Yesterday, today, for ever'

Road signs WEEK 10

Theme Life's journey
Visual aids Pictures of road signs as illustrated on page 82. A copy of the Highway Code

All wise road users, not just car drivers, should be familiar with the Highway Code. It contains all the information and instructions we need to arrive safely at our destinations. It has been called the 'road users' Bible'.

The Bible has been called the Christian's Highway Code. We are travelling on an exciting journey through life but there are many hazards, dangers and pit-falls which we will be able to avoid if we study and obey God's rules, contained in His Highway Code. Just as there are warning signposts and signals on our roads, which are illustrated in the 'Code', so there are clear warning signs in the Bible which tell us where we are going wrong and how we should live our lives. We shall see how similar God's signposts are to the ones in the Highway Code. (*Show some or all of the road signs, as follows.*)

1 This sign warns the motorist that there may be wild animals on the road. Some people behave like wild animals, too, such as football hooligans, vandals and muggers. We are warned about these people in the Bible (*2 Timothy 3, 1–5*) and are told not to be taken in by them. We are also taught not to behave like them but rather to 'do unto others as you would have them do unto you.'
2 Can you see the skid marks made by this car? The sign warns that the road is very slippery. When people don't behave properly, when they are lazy or disobedient, for example, they are said to be on a 'slippery path' which could lead to disaster for them and for other people.
3 Our next sign says *Give way* to traffic on the major road. There are times in life when we *should* give way and times when we should *not*. When we are being obstinate and stupid it is wise for us to give way to reason and sense. On the other hand, we should never give way to temptation when others seek to lead us astray.
4 We do well to obey the *Stop* sign. There are times when we should stop and think before we act rather than just rush into a situation without thought. So often we regret doing things – perhaps we have retaliated when someone has done or said something to offend, or we have jumped straight into trouble and only made

matters worse. How much better it is if we stop and think first before we act.
5 At the crossroads the motorist has to make up his mind which way to go. Frequently, in our lives, we come to a crossroads and have to choose which road to take. For example, we must choose whether to follow good advice or whether to allow ourselves to be tempted into wrong-doing. When we pray we can ask God to help us make the right decisions. We can choose to travel God's way or to travel the way of the world.
6 This sign warns that the road narrows. God's road is called a narrow road (*see Matthew 7, 13*): 'Broad is the way which leads to destruction and many there be who travel that way, but narrow is the way which leads to life and few there be that find it.' Don't just travel with the crowd. Have the courage to stand up for what you know to be right and do what God would have you do.
7 Drivers must take care when they see this sign for there could be children crossing. This sign reminds us that Jesus cared for little children and in fact said that grown ups should be like little children and have the same faith. Listen now to what Jesus said about children:

Reading   Matthew 18, 1–6

8 Finally, this sign tells a motorist that he is not allowed to stop. For those who serve God or follow Jesus Christ there should be no stopping, no turning back. Our Lord said that if we turn back we are not fit for the Kingdom (Luke 9, 62). We must 'Ever follow that which is good' (1 Thessalonians 5, 15).

Prayer   No 11
Hymns   'Saviour, teach me day by day'
          'Follow, follow, I would follow Jesus'
          'One more step'

Wild animals

Slippery road

Give way to traffic on major road

Stop and Give Way

Cross roads

Road narrows on both sides

Children

No stopping ("Clearway")

Time

WEEK 11

Aim   To encourage the wise use of time
Reading   Ecclesiastes 3, 1–9, 11a

'There is a right time for everything.'

Everything we do is governed by time. We have a 'timetable' at school. Athletes, swimmers etc are very conscious that they should strive to achieve a better time, a faster time. Some people wish that time would pass quicker. They say, 'I suppose it will pass an hour' or 'It will help to get the morning over'. This attitude is very sad; these people don't realise how exciting life can be and how much there is to be done.

Do you remember how long journeys seemed to take when you were small? You probably asked 'How long will it be before we get there?' long before you reached your destination. The older you get, the quicker time seems to fly past. I'm always asking myself, 'How can I do all the things I have planned to do?'

This experience is brought home to us in the following poem which can be seen on a clock in Chester Cathedral:

'When as a child I laughed and wept, time crept;
When as a youth I dreamed and talked, time walked;
When I became a full grown man, time ran;
And later as I older grew, time flew.
Soon I shall find while travelling on, time gone.
Will Christ have saved my soul by then? Amen

All too often, former pupils come back to school and say, 'I wish I had my time all over again. I would have tried harder'. For them, time has gone; it is often too late; they have thrown away their chance.

Think about that reading from the book of Ecclesiastes with which we began. We can make it even more applicable to our school life, eg

There is a right time for everything
A time to work hard
A time to relax and play
A time to listen to good advice
A time to act upon it
A time to speak for what we know to be right
A time to be silent and say nothing
A time to ask for help
A time to offer a helping hand

I hope you will always heed good advice and never have to say 'I wish I had my time to go over again.'

Prayer No 14
Hymn 'Fight the good fight'
  'God is working His purpose out'

Time

What is time, this abstract feeling, transient as the clouds above?
Here today but gone tomorrow,
Time for joy and time for sorrow;
Time is past and yet the future looms before with time to spare.

Time in childhood lingers on; golden hours with nought but play
Youth approaches with delight,
Time to stretch his wings in flight,
The world has opened all its doors and God has given the will to choose.

Time has grown mercurial wings, days rush by with tasks undone,
Time for us was Heaven sent
Can we say 'twas wisely spent?
Will our work unfinished be when our maker calls us home?

B.J. Wilcock

Names

WEEK 12

Theme   Being a Christian or simply having a good name
Visual aid   Several flash cards with surnames and nicknames

Have your friends given you a nickname? It is usually a mark of affection when others give you a nickname – (though not always).

For example Jonathan Smith may be known as 'Smithie' or
             Andrew Robinson may be called 'Robbo' or
             Sarah Boston may be known as 'Boz'.
(*Here the presenter could substitute nicknames well known in school.*)

Surnames are often shortened in this way to create a nickname. The origin of people's surnames is in itself an interesting study, for surnames were added later to people's 'Christian' or first names. For example, there may have been two people with the name David living in a village, one a weaver and the other a carter. To distinguish the two Davids, one was known as David Weaver, the other as David Carter. Their trades were their surnames. Can you think of any others? Here are some examples:

    Glover
    Fuller
    Cooper
    Wright
    Carter
    Weaver
    Miller
    Fisher   etc.

Another way of distinguishing two people with the same name, say Molly, was to add a description of where she lived. One Molly may have lived at the top end of the village and was called Molly Topham while the other may have lived at the bottom of a hill and was known as Molly Underhill. So we also get surnames like:

    Townsend
    Underwood
    Marsh
    Meadows   etc.

Yet another way of distinguishing people of the same name was to use their father's name, eg:

Tim William's son, which soon became Williamson
Tim Richardson
Tim Jackson
Tim Wilson
Tim Robertson
Tim Davidson

Surnames and nicknames are names which are added to your own name.

If a person has a good reputation we say that he or she 'has a good name'. Most often, people gain 'a good name' by being reliable, trustworthy, helpful, punctual, hardworking . . . for many years. But it can be ruined by a moment's thoughtlessness. We must always do our very best to ensure that our own good name – and that of our school – is not spoiled by anything we do or say.

Christian application

The disciples of Jesus had a nickname which was added in a similar way. There were called *Christ*ians. The disciples were first called Christians at Antioch (Acts 11, 26). Other people could see by their actions and by what they said that they were followers of the Lord Jesus Christ and that they had committed themselves to serving him.

We too should be pleased to bear the nickname CHRISTIAN.

(See page 88 for reading, prayer and hymn suggestions.)

Names 2

WEEK 13

Aim   To show why Jesus came
Visual aids   Several flash cards, each with a Christian name on the front and its meaning on the reverse eg

PHILIP	LOVER OF HORSES

Today we are going to think about 'Christian' names or, as some people call them, 'forenames' or 'first' names. Did you know that everyone's name has a special meaning? Have you discovered the meaning of your own name? There are lots of books on the subject. Here are some examples of the meanings of names which are frequently used today and some of which are no longer as popular:

Susan	*a lily*
Sylvia	*living in a wood*
Paul/Pauline	*little*
Angela (from an angel)	*a messenger*
Dorothy	*gift of God*
Pat/Patricia/Patrick	*noble*
Philip	*a lover of horses*
Stephen	*a crown*
Malcolm	*a disciple*
William	*a helmet of strength*
Timothy	*honoured of God*
John	*God is gracious*

Two boys were having a furious argument about their names. 'My name is better than yours!' 'No it isn't, yours is a stupid name,' replied the other. They very nearly came to blows.

Why not visit the library and try to find out the meaning of your own name? The chances are that it is very worthy. Then try to live up to the meaning of your name.

Christian application

There *is* one name which is better than every other name. Can you guess which it is?

It is the name Jesus. This name, too, has a special meaning. It simply means *Saviour*. When the angel appeared to Joseph and told him that Mary would have a son, he was instructed to call him JESUS 'for He shall save His people from their sins.'

Readings Matthew 1, 18–21 and
Philippians 2, 5–11
Prayer No 2
Hymns 'At the name of Jesus'
'How sweet the name of Jesus sounds'
'Jesus, name above all names'
'Hark the glad sound the Saviour comes'
(This is an advent hymn, the last line of which is appropriate to this theme.)

Weather forecasts WEEK 14

Theme Prophecies
Visual aid A football pools coupon. A weather forecast from the newspaper

Have you ever tried to forecast what will happen in the future? Did events turn out as you expected?

Every week many adults make a forecast. They fill in their football pools coupon, trying to forecast the results of the football matches to be played that weekend, in the hope that they will win thousands of pounds. For every person who is successful, because he has made the right forecast, there are thousands who lose.

Most people are not able to predict exactly what will happen even a few days in advance.

Another form of forecasting, which we see on the television every day or read in our newspapers, is the weather forecast. How often we see the weather men begin by admitting that they had got it wrong! Frequently, however, they are right, or at least partly right. This is because they use up-to-date scientific equipment in weather stations all over the world and in satellites to help them forecast the weather.

Whenever there is going to be a general election or a by-election, the pollsters start making predictions as to which political party is ahead. Sometimes they are right. Often they are wrong. Frequently one poll forecasts victory for one party, while another comes out with a completely different forecast.

No-one can predict the future. Of course, we should all plan ahead and make careful preparations – for a coming event, an examination or our future careers. But we should also be ready to cope with unexpected difficulties or changes in our plans. As well as thinking of the future, we need to 'live one day at a time'.

Christian application

Finally, let me tell you of some forecasts which were made hundreds of years before an event and yet they turned out to be remarkably accurate. They are the forecasts or prophecies in the Old Testament about the coming of the promised Messiah – the birth of Jesus. Make no mistake, the coming of Jesus is a historical fact. God's people had been looking forward in eager anticipation for it to happen and when it did, it fulfilled exactly Isaiah's prophecy.

90 Through the Year

Reading Isaiah 9, 6 and 7, 40. 1–5.
(See also Isaiah 53, which Christians believe to be a prophecy of the events of Easter.)
Prayer No 22
Hymn 'Hark, the herald angels sing'
'It came upon the midnight clear'
'Come and praise the Lord our King'

Santa

WEEK 15

Theme   Generosity
Visual aids   Flash cards to illustrate the origins of Father Christmas

Do you believe in Father Christmas? The answer to this question should be 'Yes'! There *was* a real Father Christmas many years ago. Today, however, anyone can be a Father Christmas.

It all started in the fourth or fifth century in Asia. Bishop Nicholas of Myrna had a reputation for helping people and doing good deeds. On one occasion he heard of the plight of three sisters whose father was so poor that he could not afford for them to get married. He had no money for the dowry which had to be paid to the husband at the time of marrying.

One night Bishop Nicholas went quietly to the house where the three girls lived with their father. He dropped a bag of gold through the window without being seen. The next morning the eldest girl was delighted. It meant she could now get married.

A second visit brought an equally pleasant surprise for the second girl. But who was the mysterious benefactor? The girls' father was determined to find out. For several nights he lay in wait and when Bishop Nicholas paid his third visit the secret was out.

As recognition for these and similar good deeds the Bishop was made a Saint – Saint Nicholas. Since that time his name has been associated with the giving of presents.

Many years later, in the seventeenth century, Dutch Protestant settlers landed in America at the place we now call New York. They tried to follow the example of Saint Nicholas, especially at Christmas time, by giving presents to each other. However, they called his name Sinter Claes which has since been changed slightly to become Santa Claus or, as he is popularly named, Father Christmas. So we see that:

BISHOP NICHOLAS	became
SAINT NICHOLAS	who became
SINTER CLAES	or
SINTER KLAAS	and then
SANTA CLAUS	alias
FATHER CHRISTMAS	

Little children think of Father Christmas as a kindly old gentleman with a white beard and red gown who climbs down chimneys with a sack full of toys on Chrimas Eve. We know, of course, that anyone can be a Father Christmas if they are kind and helpful and generous towards other people.

Christian application

As we give gifts to our friends and loved ones at Christmas time we should also give thanks to our Heavenly Father for the greatest gift of all, the gift of His son, Jesus, who became our Saviour.

The Wise Men brought their gifts to Jesus when they went to worship him. As we worship the Christ Child this Christmas time we too should bring our gifts: 'We'll bring Him hearts that love Him.'

Reading   Matthew 2, 1–11
Prayer   No 33
Hymns   'Love came down at Christmas'
         'The wise may bring their learning'
         'The Virgin Mary had a baby boy'

Janus
WEEK 1

Theme Looking backwards and forwards
Visual aid Picture of the Roman god, Janus

None of us likes a person who is two-faced. Such a person says one thing but does another. They cannot be relied upon.

In the case of Janus it was different. Janus was a Roman God who was depicted as having two faces for a very special reason. With one face he could look back to the year which had passed. His other face looked to the future. In his hand he also held a key, with which to open the new year. In AD 1582 Pope Gregory XIII introduced the calendar we use today. January 1st was made New Year's Day because it had been so in Ancient Roman times. We get the name of the first month of the year, January, from the Roman god Janus.

As we look back on the past we should not regret the year that has now gone. Neither should we wish that we could 'put the clock back'. There is little purpose in trying to live in the past. Instead, we should look back with happy memories and thank God for all we have been able to do and achieve with His help.

As we look forward to the year ahead and to the future we should do so with a spirit of eager anticipation, with determination and resolution.

> Let us resolve not to repeat any of the mistakes made last year.
> Let us resolve to do our very best work in the year ahead.
> Let us resolve to take every opportunity of helping others.
> Let us resolve never to hurt, harm or offend people.

If we all keep these resolutions the New Year will be happy and successful for everyone.

Reading Philippians 4, 4–8
Prayer No 10
Hymn 'O happy band of pilgrims'
  'Father I place into your hands'

Thin ice WEEK 2

Aim   To show how wise it is to heed warnings
Visual aid   Sign with the words: 'Beware! Thin ice'

Darren was on his way home from school one bitterly cold winter's day. He always passed near by the flooded quarry but never ventured too close. His mother had warned him of the danger of the deep water. But on this occasion he noticed several of his school pals skating on the ice. The pond had frozen over in the frosty weather. 'Come on, it's great' his friends called out to him. So Darren ventured out on to the ice.

It was great! Much better than the slides they had made on the school playground. Darren joined in the excitement. He didn't notice that he was going further out towards the middle of the pond, away from the edge of the quarry where the others were skating.

'Darren, be careful,' shouted one friend, 'you're skating on thin ice!' Just then Darren heard a loud cracking sound. He felt the ice tremble beneath his feet. Before he could do anything about it he had fallen through. At first he tried frantically to scramble out of the icy water but very quickly the intense cold overtook him and he went limp. Darren had been skating on ice which hadn't really frozen hard enough to support his weight.

Fortunately a group of men working nearby saw what happened. With the aid of a rope and a plank of wood, they managed to haul Darren out of the water. Someone called for an ambulance. The men laid Darren on the ground and wrapped him in their coats and began to revive him, restoring his circulation. When he came round, Darren noticed a signpost placed near the edge of the quarry. It read 'Beware! Thin ice'.

That story had a happy ending, but every winter we read about children who are not as fortunate as Darren and go skating on thin ice with disastrous consequences. Always remember to look out for warning signs, and ask your parents' advice.

The expression 'skating on thin ice' can be applied to other situations as well. A person who continually ignores good advice and repeatedly behaves in an unacceptable way could be said to be 'skating on thin ice'. Before very long the imaginary ice will give way and he will find himself in trouble.

Here is an example: Your teacher may say 'When I am speaking to the class, I expect you to pay attention'. Later, the teacher may say, 'I warn you, you are skating on thin ice; I heard you talking again'. Finally, your teacher may lose patience: 'Because you persistently talk instead of getting on with your work I am going to set you some extra work to do.'

Always heed the warnings.

Reading Proverbs 3, 1–12
Prayer No 13
Hymn 'The King of Love my Shepherd is'
'Dear Lord and Father of mankind'

96 *Through the Year*

Maths (1) *WEEK 3*

Theme How we should behave
Visual aids Two sheets with 'sums'

Today we are going to have a maths lesson with a difference. I'm sure you can all do simple addition like this.

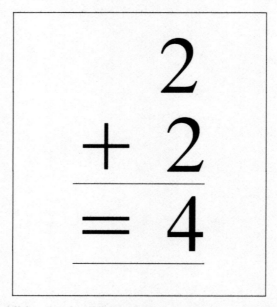

There is an addition in the Bible which is much more difficult:

Reading 2 Peter 1, 3–8 (Use the Authorised Version if possible.)

There are a lot of difficult words here, so let me explain.
A person who believes in God and follows the teaching and example of the Lord Jesus Christ can be said to have *faith*. This is only a start, though. To this faith we must keep on adding things like morality and purity (other words for virtue or goodness). And we must add moderation in our behaviour which is what is meant by temperance; we must not 'overdo' things, in other words. Of course you understand what is meant when it says that we must be kind, patient and loving. All these are very worthwhile qualities which we must add to our faith. When these things are added together what do you get? The answer is 'the sort of person God wants you to be'.

```
  Faith
+ Virtue
+ Knowledge
+ Temperance
+ Patience
+ Godliness
+ Kindness
+ Charity (love)
─────────────
=    ?
```

Now, do you recognise this type of sum?

```
  3
× 3
───
= 9
```

Of course it is multiplication – all very easy, isn't it?

A multiplication is mentioned in the Acts of the Apostles: 'The word of God grew and multiplied' (*see Acts 12. 24*). This is what happened in the very early church. How much better it would be if we tried to be the sort of people God wants us to be and allowed His word to multiply so that others would come to know of His love for them.

Prayer No 30
Hymn 'Come my brothers, praise the Lord'

(*See also pages 145–146 for additional material on this theme.*)

Year 2, Spring Term

Maths (2)

WEEK 4

Theme The basis of our faith
Visual aids More sheets with 'sums'

Today we shall continue with our maths lesson.

Here is another very simple sum:

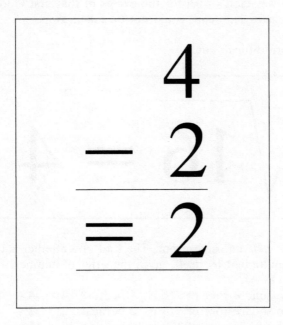

The correct name for this type of sum is a 'subtraction', though when you were much younger you may have called it a 'take away' sum. Let us now consider two 'take aways' mentioned in the Bible, one which God planned and one which could not be allowed.

1 Our first story is about John the Baptist. Huge crowds came to hear him preaching in the desert near the River Jordan. He told them that they should be sorry for the wrong that they had done, and that the Kingdom of God was very near. He also explained that he was simply preparing the way for someone very special. Suddenly John stopped and pointed: that special person had arrived. It was Jesus. John turned to Jesus and said to the people:

'Behold the Lamb of God who TAKES AWAY the sins of the world.'
2 And now the 'take away' which could not be allowed. Jesus was nearing the end of his time on earth. He was about to go to Jerusalem where he knew he would be taken captive and crucified. In preparation he went aside quietly to pray and said, 'Father if it be possible, take away this cup from me. Nevertheless not what I will but your will be done'. Jesus asked his heavenly Father to take away his suffering but also promised to do his Father's will. But it was God's wish for the events of that first Good Friday to take place. The 'cup' could not be taken away.

Here is a more difficult sum:

$$\sqrt{16} = 4$$

This is what is called a square root. The root of a number is that number which when multiplied by itself, gives the original number.

Thus the square root of 16 is 4 because 4 × 4 = 16
Thus the square root of   4 is 2 because 2 × 2 =   4
Thus the square root of 100 is 10 because 10 × 10 = 100

Every number has a root but some are difficult to work out, eg the square root of 23 is 4.7958315 but you would need a calculator or a set of log tables to find the answer.

The root of anything is something which is very basic or fundamental. We are told in the Bible that the root of all the evil in the world is the 'love of money'. We are also told who is the root of our faith. It is Jesus himself. Jesus is the name which is above every name.

Reading   Philippians 2, 1–11
Prayer   No 21
Hymns   'There is a green hill far away'
            'Seek ye first the kingdom of God'

Sine cera   WEEK 5

Aim   To illustrate the meaning of, and need for, sincerity
Visual aids   Two cards with the words: 'Sine' and 'Cera'

How good are you at writing letters?
Do you know how to start and finish a letter?

If you are writing to a very close friend or a relative you will start with the person's name – 'Dear Susan,' and you will finish off by writing 'Love from Jayne'. On the other hand, if it is a formal letter and you don't know the person's name, you should begin: 'Dear Sir or Madam' and at the end sign 'Yours faithfully, J. Brown'. Most letters to casual acquaintances would begin, 'Dear . . .' and conclude with 'Yours sincerely . . .'.

How many of you have ever ended a letter with 'Yours sincerely'? It is the most common ending to a letter but perhaps you have never realised what you have written.

The word *sincere* comes from two Latin words –

Sine which means WITHOUT and
Cera which means WAX

So now you know what you have been writing: 'Yours without wax, John Smith'.

There are two interesting theories about the origin of the word 'sincere'.

1. Long ago, when the ancient Roman armies had conquered the known world, the Roman soldiers used to buy items from the people whose country they now ruled. They would take paintings, pottery or sculptures home with them as souvenirs or as presents for their families. Quite a profitable trade sprang up between the inhabitants of the conquered country and the occupying Roman soldiers.

    Now it would take a potter or a sculptor, for example, many months to produce his valuable work of art and if in the final stages the article got chipped this would mean that many months of work had been wasted. Dishonest potters or sculptors developed a technique of filling in the chip or flaw with coloured wax so that a would-be purchaser could not tell at a glance that there was anything wrong. Only when they got it home and put it by a hot fire did they discover the fault because the wax would then melt in the heat.

As a safeguard against these dishonest practices the Romans started to insist on a guarantee being written out. The maker had to sign it to say that the artifact was *sine cera* – without wax, in other words the article was guaranteed to be genuine and free from flaws.

2 The second theory is more straightforward and comes from the world of bee-keeping. The best honey is absolutely free from the wax from the honey combs and all other impurities. Pure honey was, therefore, guaranteed to be *sine cera*, without wax.

The next time you sign yourself 'Yours sincerely' you are in effect saying that you mean what you say, you are free from impurities, you are faultless, you are genuine, you are sincere, sine cera, without wax.

Christian application

Jesus said, 'By this shall all men know that you are my disciples when you have love one for another'. Above all, Jesus requires of us that we are genuine, that we are sincere.

Reading Philippians 1, 10 and 11
Prayer No 19
Hymn 'God make my life a little light'
'Give me oil in my lamp'

Careless talk costs lives   WEEK 6

Aim   To stress the need for responsible behaviour
Visual aid   Copy of poster, obtainable from the Imperial War Museum (optional)

In World War II a slogan which frequently appeared on cinema screens and on hoardings was:

Careless talk costs lives

The Government of the day went to great lengths to warn people not to gossip about things just in case a spy overheard the conversation. Gossip on a train or in the corner shop might give clues to the enemy, for example:

Mrs Smith: 'Do you know, I saw a whole convoy of army trucks passing through the village this morning!'

Mrs Brown: 'Well I never, perhaps they are on the way to Portsmouth, something is about to happen, I am sure!'

During the war this sort of careless talk could give away valuable information to the enemy and result in the loss of many lives. It was most important in those days that people should think before they spoke. It still is.

People sometimes say hurtful, harmful things with little thought of the consequences. We all need to learn how to think before we speak or act – learning how to behave responsibly.

Christian application

Now listen to what the Bible says about learning to control one's tongue.

Reading   James 3, 1–5
Prayer   No 37
Hymn   'Heavenly Father may Thy blessing'

'Dig for Victory' WEEK 7

Aim   To show the need for thorough preparation
Visual aid   Wartime poster – obtainable from the Imperial War Museum (optional)

Another wartime slogan was

Dig for victory

During the war it was very difficult to trade with other parts of the world because merchant ships risked being attacked and sunk by the enemy. Imports of food were, therefore, very limited. Everyone had ration books which entitled them to the minimum amount of essential foods. To supplement their rations everyone who had a garden was encouraged to cultivate it, not to grow flowers or have nice lawns but instead to grow potatoes and vegetables. In this way people kept themselves healthy and fit, and were ready to fight for their country. Every patch of available land – sports fields, parks, gardens – was dug over, thoroughly prepared and cultivated. People were 'digging for victory'.

In times of peace we should dig for different kinds of victory. What are the victories we have to win?

- victory over temptation
- progress in combatting disease
- winning the fight against poverty
- overcoming famine and starvation
- doing our best at school and at home.

All these are victories to be won. Just as the ground has to be prepared and fertilised for growing plants, so we must not neglect thorough preparation and hard work. As we make progress with our studies, as we learn of all the needs of others in the world, as we gain a concern for and awareness of the world's problems we are, in effect, beginning to 'dig for victory'.

Christian application

Reading   Romans 12, 9–18
Prayer   No 35
Hymn   'When a knight won his spurs'
             'Who would true valour see?'

What's my line? WEEK 8

Aim   To be conscientious in all things
Visual aid   Ten cards numbered one to ten, as used in the television game *What's My Line?*

One of the most popular television programmes of all time was the game *What's My Line?* In it, a panel of experts had to guess the occupation of various challengers. The challenger first of all signed in and then performed a piece of mime or simple actions intended to help the panel to guess the contestant's job or occupation.

The panel of experts were allowed to ask the challenger ten questions to help them guess.

Today we are going to play *What's My Line?* We are going to see if we can beat the panel. The rules have been changed, however. We have to see if we can answer YES to ten questions. Are you ready?

1. Do I always try as hard as I can?
2. Do I do my homework conscientiously?
3. Am I considerate to other people?
4. Am I keen to join in school activities?
5. Am I proud to be a member of my school?
6. Do I try to keep my school tidy?
7. Am I punctual?
8. Do I always remember to bring the things I need for my lessons?
9. Do I take a pride in my appearance?
10. Do I keep all the school rules?

Did you beat the panel? If so, you will get your reward in due course. You will get a certificate! It will be in the form of a good report from school!

Christian application

1. Am I keen to be a follower of Jesus Christ?
2. Have I asked Him to be my Saviour and Friend?
3. Do I seek to do His will?
4. Do I try to love my neighbour as myself?
5. Do I try to help those less fortunate than myself?
6. Do I tell others about Jesus?
7. Do I speak to God in prayer?
8. Do I like to read the Bible?

9 Do I worship God regularly?
10 Do I like to be with other members of the church?

If we answer *yes* to these questions we will receive our reward. The Bible calls it 'a crown of life' and our Lord Jesus will say of us 'Well done thou good and faithful servant'.

Reading   Exodus 20, 1–17 – the Ten Commandments
Prayer   No 25
Hymn   'Saviour, teach me day by day'
         'O Jesus I have promised'

Listen! WEEK 9

Aim To demonstrate the art of good listening
Aids Cassette recorder with modern pop cassette

(Begin by playing an up-to-date pop song – preferably from the Top Ten – loudly on the cassette recorder.)

I wonder how many of you really listened to the words of that song? Probably you just enjoyed the tune and the beat of the music.

When the gramophone was first invented, families would gather in their homes to spend the evening listening intently to the latest records. Nowadays people seem to have lost the art of listening. Music blares out in our homes and our cars, even in lifts and supermarkets. We 'plug ourselves in' to personal cassette players and ear phones. We are surrounded by so much noise that few people actually sit down to listen.

Jesus was well aware that people did not always listen to what he was saying. Listen to this parable.

Reading Mark 4, 1–9. The parable of the sower

Some people are like the wayside where the seed was immediately gobbled up by the birds. This seed never even starts to grow. In other words they don't even listen in the first place.

Others, said Jesus, are like stony ground where the seed does begin to grow but soon it withers and dies because the ground is so shallow. The people who are 'shallow' very soon forget what they have been told so that it has no effect upon their lives.

Yet another category of people are like the thorny ground. They do listen but just as the thorns choke out the life of the good seed so these people allow other, less important, things to take first priority so that the words Jesus spoke have no lasting effect upon them.

But some people listened to what Jesus said and put his teaching into practice in their lives. These, Jesus said, were like good ground which yielded a good crop.

If we want to have a happy, successful time at school we must listen carefully to what we are taught. If we want to live happy and useful lives we must listen to, and obey, the teaching of Jesus.

Jesus said, 'He who has ears to hear should use them!'

Prayer No 20
Hymn 'O Jesus I have promised' (note the line *O speak and make me listen*)

Flour grader

WEEK 10

Theme   Forgiveness
Visual aid   Model or picture of a 'flour grader'

Do you recognise this person? You may have seen him at home, on a bag of flour. He is the famous Flour Grader who enters the bags of flour, punches about a bit and then throws out all the lumps, all the impurities. He has a special message for us today. It is simply: 'Get rid of the lumps'.

There are all sorts of lumps or impurities in our lives which we would be better off without. They include:

1. Selfishness – when we want the best for ourselves and are not willing to share with others.
2. Greed – when we want more than our fair share, even if it means others have to do without.
3. Jealousy – when we resent the fact that others sometimes have more than we do or seem to be more successful than we are.
4. Dishonesty – when we know we have done wrong and are reluctant to own up.
5. Laziness – when we don't put our best effort into our work.

All these 'lumps' spoil our lives and must be got rid of! Of course, there is no such person as the Flour Grader so we can't ask him to help us. But there is someone to whom we may turn, who is always ready to help – and that's God. If we ask Him, he will help us get rid of the lumps. Let us remember, however, that we can only ask God to forgive us if we are prepared to forgive others.

'And forgive us our trespasses as we forgive those that trespass against us.'

Reading   1 John 1, 5–10
Prayer   No 37
Hymn   'Looking upward every day'
            'When Jesus walked in Galilee'

If

WEEK 11

Theme Coping with setbacks.

Listen to this famous poem by Rudyard Kipling:

IF—

If you can keep your head when all about you
    Are losing theirs and blaming it on you,
If you can trust yourself when all men doubt you,
    But make allowance for their doubting too;
If you can wait and not be tired by waiting,
    Or being lied about, don't deal in lies,
Or being hated, don't give way to hating,
    And yet don't look too good, nor talk too wise:

If you can dream – and not make dreams your master;
    If you can think – and not make thoughts your aim;
If you can meet with Triumph and Disaster
    And treat those two imposters just the same;
If you can bear to hear the truth you've spoken
    Twisted by knaves to make a trap for fools,
Or watch the things you gave your life to broken,
    And stoop and build 'em up with worn-out tools:

If you can make one heap of all your winnings
    And risk it on one turn of pitch-and-toss,
And lose, and start again at your beginnings
    And never breathe a word about your loss;
If you can force your heart and nerve and sinew
    To serve your turn long after they are gone,
And so hold on when there is nothing in you
    Except the Will which says to them: 'Hold on!'

If you can talk with crowds and keep your virtue,
    Or walk with Kings – nor lose the common touch,
If neither foes nor loving friends can hurt you,
    If all men count with you, but none too much;
If you can fill the unforgiving minute
    With sixty seconds' worth of distance run,
Yours is the Earth and everything that's in it,
    And – which is more – you'll be a Man, my son!

I wonder if anyone here will ever play tennis in the Wimbledon Championships? Competitors who play on the centre court at Wimbledon pass through a doorway, above which are printed two lines from the famous poem we have just heard.

> 'If you can meet with Triumph and Disaster
> And treat those two imposters just the same;'

This quotation reminds all the players that in every game there will be a winner and a loser. What really matters is not whether we win or lose but that we have had the opportunity of competing in the true spirit of the tournament.

In all walks of life there will be setbacks; indeed it is often the case that for every success we may encounter several setbacks. When we receive a setback, the worst thing we can do is to give up and not try any more. If we experience a setback: in sport, in our work, or in an examination, the lesson we should learn is to be more determined in future. Even if we do not win the competition, even if we do not come top of the form, provided we know that we have tried harder than previously and that we have done our best, we should have good cause to be pleased with our results.

Christian application

Four men brought their sick friend on a stretcher to the house where Jesus was staying. They hoped that Jesus would heal him. But when they arrived at the house they had a setback. There were so many people wanting to see and hear Jesus that they couldn't get anywhere near him. What should they do now? They hadn't bargained for this setback. Should they give up? Let us listen to the story as Mark recorded it.

Reading　Mark 2, 1–12 (possibly omit verses 6–11)
　　　　　The men in the story had great faith; they were determined to overcome their setback. The result was that their friend was healed. When we begin any task we should be determined to see it through in spite of obstacles. This applies especially to following Jesus. He wants his followers to be wholehearted and determined.
Prayer　No 13 (a prayer by Dr William Barclay)
Hymn　'Stand up, stand up for Jesus'

Good memories WEEK 12

Theme Training one's memory
Visual aid A tray upon which several objects have been placed (or they could be stuck with Blu-Tac). Objects could include some of the following: pencil, watch, rubber, cassette, ruler, marble, sweet, bottle top, fork, pen, paper clip, brooch, pencil sharpener, pair of scissors, elastic band, protractor, drawing pin, match

We are going to begin our assembly today with a memory test (*show tray*). Study carefully the objects placed on the tray. You have exactly one minute. (*After one minute, cover the tray.*)

Now, put up your hands if you can remember seeing

- a bracelet?
- a piece of chocolate?
- a piece of string?
- a drawing pin?
- a coin?

Well, quite a few of you got some wrong. Of course, this is just a game, but it often pays to have a good memory.

How far back can you remember? I can remember things that happened to me when I was two – but I'm not going to tell you how long ago that was! Unfortunately, many pupils don't seem to be able to remember things they were told three weeks ago – that is why instructions have to be repeated so often. Some pupils can't even remember things for more than a couple of hours. No wonder their homework is sometimes not done properly or correctly!

Christian application

The disciple Peter remembered something which made him very sad. He had boasted that he would never let Jesus down and said that he was prepared to go to prison or even die rather than deny Jesus. Now listen to what happened.

Reading Luke 22, 54–62 (from the *Good News* Bible if possible).
It is most important that we remember Jesus' teachings and try to follow them.
Prayer No 6
Hymn 'There is a green hill far away'
'Lord Jesus Christ, you have come to us'

The greatest

WEEK 13

Aim   To encourage humility and modesty
Visual aid Card with slogan: 'I am the greatest'

There was once a very talented heavyweight world champion boxer named Muhammed Ali. Before every fight Muhammed Ali used to boast 'I am the greatest'. Now, Muhammed Ali was undoubtedly a very good heavyweight champion but can anyone really claim to be 'the greatest'?

Throughout history, famous leaders of different countries have been called 'great', such as

    Alfred the Great of England
    Alexander the Great of Greece
    Charles the Great of France
    Frederick the Great of Germany
    Peter the Great of Russia.

They were all famous for fighting great battles and conquering lands. But were these people *really* great?

The greatest person ever was not at all like this. I mean Jesus Christ, of course. Though he was the greatest he was humble enough to wash his disciples' feet. He said, 'Whoever would be the greatest must be the servant of all.'

We are *not* great when we

- lose our temper
- tell lies
- make life unpleasant for others
- easily take offence
- are jealous or envious of others

We are *not* great because

- we have a lot of money
- we own a Rolls Royce

The 'greatest' people are those who serve others.

Reading   Matthew 18, 1–5
Prayer   No 34
Hymn   'Guide me, O Thou Great Jehovah'
           'Jesus name above all names'

Easter eggs

WEEK 1

Aim   To illustrate the meaning of Easter
Visual aids   An Easter egg or picture of one. Two display cards with the words 'Eoster' and 'Easter'

Did you get any Easter eggs?
Did you eat them all?
   Have you ever paused to think why we have Easter eggs?
   The name EASTER comes from the name of the Anglo-Saxon goddess of Spring EOSTER.
   In pre-Christian times people used to celebrate the return of Spring; they would rejoice that the world was coming to life again. Just as baby chickens are born from eggs, so the whole world of nature is being re-born in spring-time, after the winter.
   Christians have a greater reason for celebrating Easter for it is the time when they remember that the Lord Jesus came to life again. This is called the Resurrection. We rejoice that Jesus was victorious over death and that His Spirit is still in the world today helping and strengthening those who have put their trust in Him.
   After the sad time of Lent and the events leading to Good Friday this is indeed great news. No wonder people want to celebrate by decorating their churches with flowers and by giving presents of Easter eggs to relatives and friends.
   The first Easter eggs were ordinary eggs which had been painted in brightly-coloured patterns. Nowadays they are chocolate eggs, of course.
   As we eat our Easter eggs, we should remember that this is a time of new life, and of re-birth.

Reading   Mark 16, 1–8
Prayer   No 29
Hymn   'Christ the Lord is risen today'
          'Alleluia, Alleluia give thanks to the risen Lord'

It's not cricket WEEK 2

Aim   To show the need for fair play
Visual aid   Card with the initials MCC

The beginning of the Summer Term heralds once again the beginning of the cricket season. Cricket is renowned for its spirit of fair play. In cricket it ought to be unthinkable for a player to question an umpire's decision – you've probably heard the expression, 'It isn't cricket'. It should be unthinkable for players of different teams to have an argument or even come to blows. You say 'Jolly bad luck' when an opponent is out, and when someone does particularly well on the opposing side you applaud and congratulate him.

One cricketer who was renowned for his fair play was Colin Cowdrey. He was destined to be a good cricketer because he was christened Michael Colin Cowdrey, so that he could have the same initials as the headquarters of cricket, the MCC. These letters stand for 'Marylebone Cricket Club' whose ground is at Lords. Not only was Cowdrey a fine cricketer, he was a good leader, well respected for his fair play. For this he was appointed Captain of the English team and led them to many triumphs.

'It isn't cricket' is a term which is now applied to other situations. If you were given three hours' homework to do you would justifiably think 'It isn't cricket'. You would think the same if you were told that the school would have a week less holiday this summer. But there are times when others might think the same of you, eg

- when homework is not done properly
- when you arrive late for lessons
- when you don't do as you are told
- when you don't tell the truth . . .

These are the times when it could be said of you 'It just isn't cricket.'

Christian application

The Bible advocates fair play, for we are told:

'Do unto others as you would have them do unto you.'

Reading   Proverbs 3, 3–8 (use the *Living Bible* if possible)
Prayer   No 17
Hymn   'Heavenly Father may Thy blessing'

Gilbert and Sullivan WEEK 3

Aim To illustrate the folly and futility of quarrelling
Visual aid A Gilbert and Sullivan record. (The assembly could begin by playing a recorded extract from one of Gilbert and Sullivan's most popular works)

From time to time talented people have combined their talents and have worked together in order to produce great musicals. For example there were Rodgers and Hammerstein and, more recently, Tim Rice and Andrew Lloyd Webber. But probably the most famous duo, whose works have remained popular for over 100 years, were Sir William Schwenk Gilbert and Sir Arthur Seymour Sullivan. They composed comic or popular light-hearted operettas. Gilbert wrote the words and Sullivan composed the music. These are some of their famous comic operas:

    The Pirates of Penzance
    Trial by Jury
    The Mikado
    HMS Pinafore
    The Gondoliers
    The Yeomen of the Guard
    Iolanthe
    Ruddigore
    Patience   to mention just a few!

Gilbert and Sullivan's first production was in 1871 and the two men worked closely together for more than 20 years. Music lovers of the time eagerly looked forward to the staging of each new operetta at the Savoy Theatre. But then came trouble. Gilbert and Sullivan had a quarrel about, of all things, a carpet. Instead of being able to discuss their problems and negotiate, they stopped working together. There were no more Gilbert and Sullivan operas. Many people were disappointed. If only they had not had that quarrel they must surely have composed many more operas. But alas it was not to be.

    Sadly, people do quarrel – often over very trivial things. It would be so much better if each party involved in a disagreement was prepared to give way a little and be ready to discuss their problems and so settle their differences.

Christian application

In his letter to the Christians in Rome, Paul says how very important it is for us to live as far as possible at peace with everyone.

Reading   Romans 12, 14–18
Prayer   No 19
Hymn   The tune of our hymn was composed by Sir Arthur Sullivan; it is called 'Onward Christian Soldiers'.

Wedding invitation WEEK 4

Aim To illustrate the necessity of being prepared
Visual aid A wedding invitation card

Have you ever received one of these? It is an invitation to a wedding. If you ever receive one, you will be involved in lots of preparations. First of all you must reply to the invitation. Then you will have to buy a suitable wedding present and maybe some new clothes.

Jesus told a story about ten girls who received an invitation to a wedding. Five of them, sadly, did not make adequate preparations.

Reading Matthew 25, 1–13

In the time of Jesus people had to travel on foot or by camel or donkey. This would take a long time. The bridegroom presumably had to travel a long way for the wedding; the guests would not even know on which precise day he was due to arrive. As long as they were well-prepared and had plenty of oil for their lamps all would be well.

But five were foolish. They did not take sufficient oil and so they had to miss out on the wedding celebrations. While they were away trying to obtain oil the bridegroom came and the door was shut and locked. Unfortunately the foolish maidens were then not able to gain entrance to the celebrations.

Here is a modern parable. Ten pupils were given some homework to do. Five were wise and five were foolish. Those who were wise did their work and handed it in on time. The five who were foolish said:

> 'I've forgotten to do it.'
> 'I've forgotten to bring it.'
> 'I didn't have time to do it.'
> 'I was too busy to do it because my cousin came from Australia.'
> 'I've not done mine because I left my notes at school.'

It is just the same in every age, in every generation. Those who are foolish, who are badly prepared are the ones who are left out. They are left behind by those who do their preparations thoroughly.

Christian application

Of course there is a far deeper meaning to this parable. Jesus is telling people to be ready for His coming by being actively engaged in doing God's work.

Prayer No 3
Hymns 'Who is on the Lord's side?'
'Mine eyes have seen the glory'
'I have decided to follow Jesus'

God is now here!   WEEK 5

Theme   God's presence – a message for Whitsuntide
Visual aid   Two cards with the words:

God is nowhere
God is now here

Mary's uncle had been very ill. Day after day he sat in his chair by the fireside, slowly recovering from his operation. It is understandable that at times he felt depressed and down-hearted. Mary visited him often and tried her best to cheer him up by playing games to exercise and occupy his mind. But one particular day he must have been feeling very low, wondering if God really cared for him. He asked Mary to get a pencil and paper to write down these words:

GOD IS NOWHERE

Painstakingly, little Mary wrote down the letters as her uncle spelt them out. She wrote them out carefully, but she did make one mistake. Mary left too large a space between the W and the H in NOWHERE so that when she took the paper over to her uncle it read exactly the opposite of what he had intended to say. The message now read:

GOD IS NOW HERE

Mary's uncle suddenly felt much better. He realised that God was with him and that he did care for him, very much.

    The message of Whitsuntide is that God is now here. Our Lord himself promised that where two or three are gathered together in His name, He will be with them in spirit. (*See Matthew 18, 20.*) Before Jesus ascended to Heaven he promised his disciples that he would not abandon them but would send his Spirit and his power to strengthen and guide them. His last words were, 'Lo! I am with you always, even to the end of the age.'

    Whitsuntide is a time in the Christian calendar when we recall that God gave His Spirit, His strength to His disciples. Christians throughout the centuries testify that God does care and does help those who put their trust in Him. He is present with them.

Reading Acts 2, 1–4 and John 14, 12–17
Prayer   No 20
Hymns   'Our blest Redeemer'
           'Come down, O Love Divine'
           'God's not dead'

Donkeys

WEEK 6

Aim To show how advantageous it is to share

Fred was getting quite old and ready for retirement. Fred was the man who owned the donkeys on . . . . beach.

He had made up his mind it was time to call it a day, so he called his three sons together and explained that he was going to share his donkeys among them so that they could carry on his business. Tom, being the eldest son, would receive half of his father's donkeys. Dick, the middle son, had also done quite a bit of work for his father, so it was decided he should have a third of the donkeys. Young Harry, the third son, would receive one ninth, as he had not worked for very long.

Everyone agreed that this was a very fair way of sharing the donkeys, so they all went off to the field to sort them out. Here they hit a snag. When they counted them they discovered there were seventeen donkeys.

This meant that Tom was entitled to $8\frac{1}{2}$ donkeys!

It was more difficult for Dick, who had to have one third, because one third of seventeen is $5\frac{2}{3}$ donkeys.

And poor young Harry had to have one ninth of 17, which came to 1.888 donkeys!

What on earth could they do now? They didn't quarrel or argue – they sat down and tried to think of a way of dividing the donkeys fairly.

Presently along came Bert Jones and he enquired what their problem was. 'I know,' said Bert, 'I have a donkey of my own, on my allotment. If it's any help you may have it'.

Now the brothers had 18 donkeys. Let's see if that made the problem easier to solve.

Tom had half of 18	= 9 donkeys
Dick had one third of 18	= 6 donkeys
Harry had one ninth of 18	= 2 donkeys
a total of	17 donkeys

and there was one donkey left over! So Bert Jones could have his donkey back.

That story was made up! But it illustrates a very important truth – that if we are prepared to share with others we never seem to lose out ourselves. In fact quite the reverse often occurs. Bert was very happy indeed to have helped the brothers solve their problem and he got his own donkey back.

Unfortunately, today, so many people are intent on getting their own rights and are not bothered about other people. They say, 'I must have my share'. They are only interested in what they can get.

The world would be a much better place if people tried to ensure that other people got their share.

Christian application

Reading Romans 12, 8(b)–13(a) R.S.V.
Prayer No 38
Hymn 'O what can little hands do?'
'God make my life a little light'
'O Lord all the world belongs to you'

Help! WEEK 7

Aim To illustrate the importance of truthfulness

Jason's trouble was that he didn't always tell the truth. One day he was swimming in a river when he spotted a man fishing on the opposite bank. 'Help! Save me! I'm drowning!' Jason shouted. Straight away the fisherman jumped into the river to rescue the boy.

Jason, however, then swam strongly to the side, climbed ashore and laughed at the man who had tried to save him.

The following weekend Jason was again swimming in the river, this time after a large meal of fish and chips. Now it is very stupid to go swimming after a large meal and Jason got stomach cramp. Seeing the same fisherman on the opposite bank he again shouted, 'Help, save me, I'm drowning!'

Guess what? This time the man took no notice and Jason drowned.

This story is told to illustrate a very important fact. If we tell lies then we, ourselves, will suffer. 'Be sure your sins will find you out!' (*Numbers 32, 23.*)

Reading Galatians 6, 1–7
Prayer   No 13
Hymn   'Heavenly Father may Thy Blessing' (Note the line 'truthful speech and honest action')

Snakes and ladders   **WEEK 8**

Aim   Coping with life's ups and downs
Visual aid A snakes and ladders board

Have you ever played *Snakes and Ladders*? When your counter lands on a ladder you can go up to a higher score. But if you land on a snake, you slide back to the beginning again. Life itself has its snakes and its ladders.

Reading   Genesis 28, 11, 12, 13(a), 15 and 16
            (Jacob's dream at Bethel)

Jacob certainly had his ups and downs! He had done a very stupid and wicked thing by deceiving his blind father Isaac. It was his elder brother, Esau, who should have received the blessing, but Jacob was jealous and so he stooped to deceit. So that his father would think it was Esau, Jacob put a goat skin on his own arm to make it feel and smell like the hairy skin of his elder brother. So Isaac mistakenly blessed Jacob. When Isaac realised he had been tricked, though he was very sad, he would not go back on his word. As for Jacob, he had to flee for his life, with a great feeling of guilt.

Feeling weary, Jacob lay down for a sleep. We have just read the account of the dream he had in which he saw a ladder reaching from earth to heaven. Jacob realised that God had spoken to him, was prepared to forgive him, had special tasks for him to do and that there were ladders to be climbed.

We, too, have ladders to climb. A football team which wins its first round match in the FA cup can be said to have climbed the first rung of a ladder which will lead the team to Wembley.

A young tennis star who wins a junior tournament could be said to have climbed the first rung of the ladder which will one day lead to the Wimbledon Championship.

When pupils do their best in examinations they climb another rung in the ladder which will lead them to success. Learning to be sociable, reliable, helpful, courteous, appreciative are ways of earning a good report from school which is another rung up the ladder to success.

But there are also hidden snakes lurking and waiting for us; snakes which spoil our lives, make us unhappy, mar our progress and hinder our work. Let's think of some 'snakes'.

   1 There is the snake called laziness which prevents us doing our
     work properly.

2 Then there are the snakes of envy and jealousy which make us fall out with our friends.
3 And there is dishonesty, lie-telling and cheating. These 'snakes' bring us back with a bump to the very beginning.

We must all strive to avoid going down snakes and instead do our best to climb ladders so that we may make a success of our career at school and of our lives.

Christian application

Let us not forget Jacob's ladder, for most important of all is to strive to do what God wants us to do.

Prayer   No 19
Hymns   'Looking upward every day'
   'We are climbing Jesus' ladder'

Beware the camel's nose   WEEK 9

Aim   To show the importance of avoiding temptation

There is an ancient Arab saying, 'Beware the camel's nose'. It is all about keeping clear of temptation.

Late one night an Arab was all alone in his tent when he heard footsteps and a rustling sound near his tent door. He looked up with a start and was surprised to see the folds of his tent door pushed aside and the nose of a camel poking through.

He was even more surprised when the camel spoke to him. 'It is so cold outside tonight. Would you mind very much if I just put my nose in through the door of your tent so that I may get it a little bit warmer?' Though he was not at all keen on the idea the Arab said, 'Well, alright, but see that you come in no further,' and so saying he went on with his work.

When the Arab next looked up the whole of the camel's head was in through the door of the tent. 'I thought I told you not to come in any further,' said the Arab. 'But my head was so cold that I thought, seeing you had let me put my nose inside your tent, you would not mind if I put my head in,' the camel replied.

'Well, see you come no further,' said the Arab, and turned again to his work.

The next time the Arab looked up he saw that the camel had his front feet inside the tent and was moving in still further. This greatly angered the Arab who took a stick and tried to force the camel out of his tent. But it was too late – the camel walked right in to the tent and sat down on the mat, saying 'If you don't like my being in the tent and sharing it with you then you had better get out and find somewhere else to live.'

The Arab's big mistake was that he did not prevent the camel putting its nose inside his tent. He should have made his stand right at the start.

BEWARE THE CAMEL'S NOSE!

The moral of the story should be clear by now. If we allow unkind thoughts to come into our minds, if we begin to do hurtful things, if we allow ourselves to be just a little dishonest we will soon find that these things grow and begin to take a more prominent part in our lives. We must take a firm stand against temptation whenever it comes our way.

Christian application

Whenever we feel tempted, we would do well to say this simple prayer, from the hymn:

> 'When I'm tempted to do wrong
> Make me steadfast, wise and strong.'

Our reading tells us how Jesus overcame temptation.

Reading   Matthew 4, 1–11
Prayer   No 30
Hymn   'Soldiers of Christ arise'

A flash in the pan

WEEK 10

Aim To encourage consistency
Visual aid Poster or picture of a musket (flintlock gun)

Whenever examination results are announced the recipients may be divided into four groups:

1 There will be many who will have done well; they will feel satisfied and will deserve praise.
2 Some will not have done quite as well but will have tried their best. These too should not be downhearted for they deserve praise.
3 There may be some who are disappointed by their results because they know they could have done better. They did not really deserve to do well. These are the ones who need to resolve to make a determined effort in future.
4 There is, however, a fourth category – those whose good results may have been unexpected. For them, their success may just have been a 'flash in the pan'.

Let us consider the expression 'A flash in the pan'. It comes from the old flintlock musket which was widely used before the development of the percussion cap or cartridge. The force which propelled the bullets in those early days was in the form of loose gunpowder. The powder was carefully measured and placed in the flash pan of the gun. A spark from the flint was then used to ignite the gunpowder. This was a very unreliable method. Often, instead of exploding the gunpowder properly the spark might just cause a fizzle or a 'flash in the pan' which soon faded out.

A flash in the pan is, therefore, some success which is very short-lived. If you have been surprised by your success, this should make you realise that you will have to work very hard to maintain your good results. If you now sit back and relax, then your good results may well turn out to be just a flash in the pan.

Christian application

Now hear what Jesus said about those whose discipleship was just a flash in the pan.

Reading Luke 9, 57–62
Prayer No 4
Hymn 'Who would true valour see'

Jewels

WEEK 11

Aim To demonstrate our value to God
Visual aid Several items of costume jewellery
Reading Malachi 3, 16–18 (Use the Authorised Version if possible)

How incredible! Apparently there are some people who are so valuable to God that He calls them (in the Authorised version) His jewels. Who are *these* people? How can *we* become God's jewels?

Malachi wrote his prophecy in about 460 BC at a time when God's people had begun to doubt His love and had begun to say that it was useless to obey His commands. But some had remained faithful. These were described as God's special possessions or His jewels.

If we are faithful to God then we too could be His jewels. But why are God's faithful people called jewels? The answer is because they are precious to Him. They are precious to God for the same reasons that jewels are precious. For example:

1 Jewels are precious because they are rare. If we could go into our back garden and dig up diamonds by the spadeful they would be worthless.

   When people turn away from God as in the time of Malachi, then those who remain faithful are rare and are, therefore, very precious.
2 Jewels are precious because they are varied. There are so many different kinds, shapes and colours of jewels. All are different. We too are different; God has given each of us different talents to use in His service and the service of our fellow men.
3 Jewels are precious because they are so costly. Men risk their lives mining diamonds or diving to the sea bed to acquire pearls. Much time and toil and skill is then required to prepare such jewels for use in brooches, necklaces, tiaras, etc. No wonder they are expensive.

God's faithful people are precious, too, because they have cost God so much. 'For God so loved the world that He sent His only begotten son that whosoever believeth in Him should not perish but have everlasting life' (John 3, 16).

This jewellery is not genuine – it is only costume jewellery and is, therefore, worthless. At a glance it appears to be the real thing but in fact it is fake jewellery. Let us beware. God is not taken in by fakes! Our love for Him must be genuine.

Prayer No 2
Hymns 'O happy band of pilgrims'
         'God knows me'

Motorway ends

Theme   Coping with life's problems
Visual aid Drawing of a 'Motorway Ends' sign

The next time you travel on a motorway I want you to look out for this sign. The sign tells you that you have at last come to the end of the motorway. No doubt many of you will be pleased to see it, because travelling on motorways can be very tedious and monotonous.

There is an end to almost everything. Let us think of the things we are glad to see the end of:

Examinations These are necessary, but not many people really enjoy them.
Illness When we have been confined to bed or to the house for some time we are pleased when the illness comes to an end.
Unpleasant tasks We sometimes say 'I'm glad to see the back of that job!' You may have heard your parents say, when things get on top of them, 'There's no end to this'. But the end does eventually come.

There are also times when we are sad that things come to an end. Can you suggest some?

School holidays seem too short for most pupils, though perhaps not for your parents!

We are sometimes sorry when a favourite television programme comes to an end.

If we are stupid enough to quarrel and fall out with a good friend, before long we will be sorry that the friendship has come to an end. Maybe we could have tried harder to be kind and sympathetic.

Even life itself one day must come to an end. This is one of the realities we have to accept. Losing a loved one is something we all have to face sooner or later.

'All good things come to an end.' We should make the best use of our talents and our opportunities and we should enjoy our friendships while we have the chance, living our lives usefully and to the full.

Today another school year comes to an end. I expect some of you may be glad about that but there will be many who are sorry.

Whatever your feelings, you should look upon it not as an end but as the beginning of the next phase of your school-life.

Christian application

It is not strictly true to say '*All* good things come to an end.' There is one good thing which is never-ending. It is God's love.

Reading   1 Corinthians 13, 4–13 – a reading about love which never ends.

Note: It is a Christian belief that our life here on earth is just a training, a preparation for a far greater life afterwards. Death itself is not the end, it is the beginning of something far more wonderful.

Prayer   No 14
Hymn   'O Jesus I have promised'

Supplement

1 Harmony

Aim To encourage a greater understanding and tolerance of others' opinions and beliefs

This morning we are going to have a music lesson.

How many of you have ever been to an orchestral concert?

How many of you have listened to an orchestral concert on the radio or television?

How many of you have been to a pop concert?

You will have noticed that, before the concert begins, all the instruments have to be tuned. In an orchestra a note called 'concert 'A'' is sounded on the oboe and all the other instruments tune in to this. Should one instrument be out of tune it will completely spoil the whole effect. It is just the same with pop groups. The guitars have to be in tune with the electronic keyboard. If they are not in the same key the result would be disastrous.

If you study music you will discover that certain notes fit together better than others. Here is a little demonstration: (*Ask the pianist to play a series of basic chords.*) These notes harmonise well; they are said to be *concordant*. But now listen to these notes. (*The pianist could now play of series of chords consisting of consecutive notes.*) These notes clash and create a very unpleasant sound; they are said to be discordant.

Have you ever heard a two-year-old child play the piano for the first time? The child usually thumps the keys and has no idea where to place each finger. The result is a horrible noise. In order to produce pleasant sounds on a musical instrument we have to learn the rules of harmony and we must be prepared to put in years of practice.

One of the most important lessons we have to learn as we grow up is how to live harmoniously with one another. People of different races, of different colour and of different religions must learn how to respect each other's views and do nothing which would spoil their relationships. It is very sad if in a school, for example, pupils taunt each other because of their differences.

Just as there are many different instruments in an orchestra and each has to be in tune with the others, so it is in our school community. We all have different talents and make different contributions to the life of the school. For everyone's well-being we must live harmoniously.

Christian application

The Bible contains lots of advice on how we should respect and treat other people. Here are two such examples:

Readings   Hebrews 13, 1–2: 'Let brotherly love continue. Do not neglect to show hospitality to strangers.'
              Romans 12, 9, 10 and 16: 'Let love be genuine; hate what is evil, hold fast to what is good; love one another with brotherly affection; outdo one another in showing honour.'
Prayer   No 26
Hymn   'In Christ there is no East or West'

2 The big fight

Aim   To create an awareness of the plight of many in developing countries and to show what could be done to alleviate suffering

I want to tell you this morning about the Big Fight. What do you think I mean?

No, I'm not going to tell you about a certain group of young people who are frequently in trouble for using their fists in a mistaken attempt to sort out their differences.

Perhaps you think I'm going to talk about the recent championship boxing contest between ..... and ....., which was screened on television and given a great build-up in the press. This, you recall, was labelled 'The Big Fight'.

Or could I be recalling one of the classic contests of the past . . .

BRUNO v TYSON
or MUHAMMED ALI v HENRY COOPER

Again you would be wrong!

I refer this morning to a 'big fight' in which we should all be involved. It is the fight against poverty and injustice.

Don't you think it is scandalous that half the people of the world have far more food than they need; far more than is good for them, while the other half are starving to death? We frequently see scenes on the television news of people in developing countries, for example in parts of India, or in Ethiopia or Sudan who have become victims of serious droughts and famines and have been stricken with terrible diseases. How sad it is to see pictures of little children with their thin arms outstretched pleading for food. These people are in desperate need of medical supplies and food. Their nations need educating in the techniques of good farming and good planning.

This battle against hunger, starvation, famine, poverty and ignorance is a fight which must be fought and won. It is 'The big fight'. We can all become involved in this task by contributing to appeals and charity fund raising. (*Mention any current project.*)

Christian application

Jesus teaches that we should have compassion and concern for those who are less fortunate than we are. He made it clear that when we help those in need we are pleasing him.

Reading Matthew 25, 34–40
Prayer No 34
Hymn 'When I needed a neighbour were you there?'

3 Trees

Theme Conservation
Visual aid Any picture of a tree or a woodland scene

This morning we are going to consider what the world would be like if there were no trees.

If there were no trees – what would we *not* have?

Answers

1 No timber to use for fuel.
2 No timber to use for building.
3 No wood to use for making furniture.
4 There would be no homes for birds, and we need birds to eat harmful insects which would destroy crops.
5 We would not have so much fertile ground. People have learned from their mistakes in the past that if trees and hedgerows are removed then there is nothing to prevent strong winds from blowing away the top soil. In some parts of the world the removal of trees has actually created deserts. In other areas trees have been

removed from hillsides – the rain then falls on the hills but because there are no trees to drink the water, the surrounding countryside becomes flooded. You can see how much water the trees soak up if you plant a willow tree in a flooded garden. The problem will soon be cleared up.
6 Finally, without trees we would find it very difficult to live. We rely upon the trees to take in through their leaves some of the gases in the atmosphere which would be harmful to humans.

We should have every sympathy with, and give our support to, those who are trying to conserve or preserve our woodlands and forests. We have a duty to future generations.

In the reign of Queen Elizabeth I Britain had vast areas of oak forests. These were cut down to make sailing ships and to build great halls and mansions. No-one thought to plant young trees for the benefit of future generations so that today the oak forests have largely disappeared. This is what happens when one generation doesn't think ahead and plan for the future. We all have a responsibility to look after our countryside and see that it is not spoiled for future generations.

Christian application

The Bible tells us that when God created the world he first made sure that everything had been provided which would be needed by man and this included trees. He then gave to man the responsibility of caring for the environment.

Reading   Genesis 1, 27–31
Prayer   No 24
Hymn   'For the beauty of the earth'

4 Water

Theme   Conservation
Visual aid   Tumbler of water

When two adults meet in the street the ensuing conversation is invariably about the weather. A warm, sunny day makes people feel happy and friendly, but a dull, rainy day often has the opposite effect.

We all tend to grumble when it rains, particularly if we were going out for the day or going to play tennis or cricket or golf, or any other outdoor pursuit.

This morning I want you to consider how fortunate we are that in our country we get a lot of rain. Without rain there would be no water in the taps. We would turn on the taps and nothing would happen.

Without water, we would have nothing to quench our thirst; don't think that we could drink milk instead because without water the cows which provide the milk would die.

Without water we would not be able to wash our hands and faces or necks! Some of you may feel that that would be a good thing! Perhaps you would have preferred to have lived in the time of Queen Elizabeth I. It was said of her that she had a bath four times a year whether she needed it or not! People in those days didn't have the same methods of keeping clean or the same standards of hygiene as we have today.

But water is not only needed for cleanliness; it is not just necessary to quench our thirst. It is necessary to sustain life itself. When there is a drought, a lack of water, the crops fail and there is no food to eat.

There are several lessons for us to learn. Don't grumble about the rain: we are indeed fortunate to live in a country where there is plenty of water. Don't waste water: it is a very valuable commodity. Always turn off taps.

Let us think today about those people who live in countries where there is drought, where there is no water to drink or to wash and where crops have again failed due to lack of rain. (Refer to any current crisis being reported on the television and in the newspapers.)

Christian application

Jesus said that the help, strength and power he can give to us is like *living water*. This is what he said to the woman of Samaria who came to the well to draw water.

Reading   John 4, 7–14
Prayers   Nos 24 and 34
Hymn   'All things bright and beautiful'

5   Disasters

Hymn   'O God our help in ages past'
        'The Lord's my Shepherd'
        'The King of Love my Shepherd is'
        'How sweet the name of Jesus sounds'

Throughout the ages, in every period of history, there have been disasters. You may have learned in your history lessons of the Great Plague of London in 1665. It was closely followed by the Great Fire of London which destroyed most of that great city.

Many disasters have occurred during travel. One of the most famous was the sinking of the Titanic, a British White Star liner which was supposed to have unsinkable. Yet this great ship struck an iceberg off the Grand Banks of Newfoundland in April 1912 and all told, 1513 lives were lost. This disaster has been the subject of several films.

Air travel has also been marked by disaster. One of the earliest forms of air travel was by airship, that is, a power-driven balloon filled with highly inflammable gas. The destruction of the R101 in 1930 marked the end of airship building in Britain. The spectacular explosion of the Hindenburg in 1937 at Lakehurst, New Jersey, marked the end of airship travel by the German nation. In more recent times we have had several disasters involving huge jet airliners, some of the accidents, alas, the result of sabotage. Nevertheless, air travel is still thought to be one of the safest forms of travel and vast number of passengers fly safely every day.

One of the saddest disasters was that which occurred at Aberfan, a small mining village in Mid Glamorgan. In 1966 a colliery tip slipped and the resulting avalanche buried the local school and many of the homes. Of the 144 people who died 116 were children.

Now we have just heard of the disaster at . . . . . (*Give brief details as appropriate.*)

Inevitably, we ask Why do these things happen? Why do innocent people have to get injured and even die? There are no real answers to these questions. It doesn't seem to make things any easier to point out that most disasters happen because of human mistakes or even as a result of the foolish or inhuman actions of people. But our thoughts and our sympathy are extended today to all who are suffering and to all who have been bereaved. Let us now remember them in our prayers:

> O God our loving Father we pray today for all who are suffering as a result of the terrible disaster at . . . . . We think of those who have been injured and also those who have lost loved ones. Father we ask you to comfort and sustain them in their time of suffering and sorrow. We pray that you will give your strength to the medical teams and the rescue teams that they may be able to bring relief to the victims. In time we pray, Lord, that all who suffer may be given your peace. This our prayer we ask through Jesus Christ our Lord. Amen.

The Lord's Prayer.

The Grace of the Lord Jesus Christ, the love of God and the fellowship of the Holy Spirit be with us all, evermore. Amen.

6 Red spot

Aim   To encourage an awareness of the world around us and to take a closer look at ourselves
Visual aid   A sheet of plain, white paper with a red spot in the centre

Today we begin our assembly by carrying out a little experiment. Put up your hands if you would like to tell me what you can see. (*Hold up the paper. In the event of someone giving the correct answer, the presenter could say 'well done', and continue.*)

Most people would say that they could see a spot or a red spot. Let me tell you what I can see. I can see a sheet of plain, white paper with a red spot in the centre.

The point of the experiment is to show that we are sometimes tricked into seeing just a small detail and do not notice what is around us. When something bad happens, we think 'What a terrible world it is'. But we should look more carefully and see the good in people and the wonder of the world in which we live. There is a tendency for us to see the small fault in another person and not recognise the large fault in our own lives.

Christian application

Jesus gives us this warning. 'How can you see to remove a speck of sawdust from your friend's eye if you have a plank of wood in your own eye?' In other words, we should not be always on the look out for faults in other people for we ourselves may well have far greater faults.

Reading   Matthew 7, 1–5
Prayer   No 26
Hymn   'Stand up, clap hands, shout thank you Lord'

7 Lost property

Aim   To encourage a sense of responsibility
Visual aid The school lost property box

We are going to begin our assembly today by carrying out a survey. I want you to put up your hand if you can think of something which often gets lost.

Here are some typical examples:

- pen
- dinner money
- purse
- tie
- homework book
- bus fare
- games kit
- friends
- your temper
- your way

The obvious thing to do if ever you lose something is to search thoroughly for it. Jesus told a story about a woman who had ten pieces of silver and lost one of them. She did the sensible thing. She got a lamp and a broom and swept out the whole house until she found the lost coin. When she found it she and her neighbours had a little celebration.

Sometimes we get lost ourselves. You may remember, when you were much younger, getting lost in a large department store or on a crowded beach. It was a frightening experience.

People sometimes lose their way in life. They wander away from God like a sheep sometimes wanders away from the flock. It is important for us to remember that Jesus said he was like a good shepherd who cares for the sheep. If we follow his example and teaching we will never lose our way.

Reading   Luke 15, 8–10
Prayer   No 1
Hymn   'Lord of the dance'

8 Ice buns

Aim   To give an insight into the harsh realities of war and show the folly of warfare
Visual aid   One small bar of chocolate

The lady from next door was knocking furiously on the front door. When the door was eventually opened she shouted excitedly, 'They've got ice buns at Chester Bakery'. (*Here substitute the name of a long-established local confectioners.*)

'So what?' you would say, 'Of course they've got ice buns, they always have, and lots of other cakes and very good they are too'. But you see this was not always so. The incident to which I referred happened during the last world war, during the years from 1939 to 1945 when most countries of the world were fighting each other. Let me describe what life was like.

First of all there were hardly any cakes in the shops. If there were a few cakes for sale the news would spread rapidly from house to house and a large queue would form along the street outside the cake shop. Neither were there any sweets – not until rationing was introduced and everyone was given a ration book. This entitled each person to buy one small bar of chocolate, like this, each week. The reason for rationing was that food was in very short supply because sugar, grain and other foods had to be brought by sea from other countries. Enemy submarines lay in wait below the surface of the sea ready to fire torpedoes at merchant ships in order to sink them. Everything had to be rationed: food, sweets, clothes and even furniture.

When pupils went to school in those days they had to be sure to take their gas masks with them. These they carried in cardboard boxes hung around their necks. At school they would be shown how to put their gas masks on, covering their faces as a precaution in case the enemy decided to drop gas bombs. Frequently a loud wailing sound would be heard. This air raid siren was a warning to everyone that enemy aeroplanes had been sighted. Everyone quickly made their way to underground air raid shelters where they had to remain in a dimly-lit, stuffy atmosphere until the 'All Clear' was sounded. Sadly for some when they emerged from the shelter they would find that their school was just a smoking pile of rubble, destroyed by enemy bombs. Even worse, some would discover when they returned home, that their homes had been bombed and relatives injured or even killed.

Today we are used to our streets and towns being brightly lit. Neon advertising signs show us where the theatres, restaurants and amusement halls are located. Not so during the war. There had to be a total black out. Black curtains or paper had to be used at all the windows. No light could be allowed to show as this might guide enemy aeroplanes and show them where to drop their bombs.

What a terrible thing war is, and how futile. There can never be any real winners. To-day the nuclear weapons which nations could use are infinitely more powerful than the weapons used in the last world war. How important it is that the leaders of the nations should learn to settle their differences by negotiation and not by war.

Christian application

Jesus said 'Blessed are the peacemakers for they shall be called the sons of God'. In our reading the prophet Isaiah looks forward to a time when people will have learned to live in peace.

Reading   Isaiah 2, 1–4
Prayer   No 3
Hymn   'Heavenly Father may thy blessing'

9 Pied Piper

Theme   Be as good as your word

The people of Hamlin were very worried. A plague of rats had infested their homes. In desperation the Mayor of Hamlin offered a substantial reward to anyone who could rid the town of this terrible plague of rats. Along came the Pied Piper who claimed he could do just what the Mayor requested. He was given the job. As soon as he began to play a tune on his pipes the rats began to come out of their holes and follow the Piper.

Here is a wonderful description from the poem *The Pied Piper of Hamlin* written by Robert Browning.

> To blow the pipe his lips he wrinkled,
> And green and blue his sharp eyes twinkled
> Like a candle-flame where salt is sprinkled;
> And ere three shrill notes the pipe uttered,
> You heard as if an army muttered;
> And the grumbling grew to a mighty rumbling;
> And out of the houses the rats came tumbling.
> Great rats, small rats, lean rats, brawny rats,
> Brown rats, black rats, grey rats, tawny rats,
> Grave old plodders, gay young friskers,
> Fathers, mothers, uncles, cousins,

Cocking tails and pricking whiskers,
Families by tens and dozens,
Brothers, sisters, husbands, wives –
Followed the Piper for their lives.
From street to street he piped advancing,
And step for step they followed dancing,
Until they came to the river Weser
Wherein all plunged and perished!

The Piper led the rats out of the town until they all drowned in the river. Having completed his task he returned to claim his reward. But the Mayor, now seeing that the rats had all gone, changed his mind. In his anger the Pied Piper began to play his tune again and this time all the children of the town followed the Piper, never to return. All except one lame boy who was not able to keep up with the others. The Mayor had broken his promise. The result was disastrous for the town of Hamlin.

It used to be said of Englishmen, by foreigners, that 'An Englishman's word was his bond'. This does not always seem to be the case these days. So many people seem unreliable and go back on their word. If we have any sense we will not deal with a company or a salesperson who by deceit provides us with faulty goods. Neither would we repeat, for example, a holiday booking with a travel firm whose advertising information we discover to be misleading.

For our part we should work hard to build for ourselves a good reputation for honesty and reliability so that others will come to know that we are as good as our word.

An original version of *The Pied Piper* ends with the line 'If we've promised them aught, let us keep our promise'.

Reading   Ephesians 5, 6–10
Prayer   No 37
Hymn   'O Jesus I have promised'

10   Maths 3

Themes   Avoiding divisions; learning to share
Visual aid Sheet with simple division (illustrated)

$$8 \div 2 = 4$$

You will all know that this simple sum is called a *division*. The larger figure is divided into smaller groups. When pupils can't get on together in a class, when there are quarrels which cause them to fall out, we say there are divisions. What should be a happy and united form has become divided into smaller groups who can't get on with each other. This is a very sad state of affairs. It is even sadder when there are divisions in families, divisions between nations and races and even divisions in churches.

It is God's wish that we should not be divided and Jesus prayed that we might all be one.

Another name for a division sum is *Sharing*. You will probably have used this name when you were at primary school. In many ways I think it is a better name. In our sum if 8 is shared equally between 2 groups each group would have 4.

It is most important that, as we grow up, we learn how to share with others.

Jesus was able to do wonderful things when people were prepared to share what they had.

Reading   John 6, 1–14 – The feeding of the five thousand

Many people today are intent on seeing to it that they get their share. The followers of Jesus Christ have a different outlook. They should see to it that other people get *their* share.

Prayer   No 18 or 19
Hymn   'Onward Christian Soldiers' (Note the line 'we are not divided')

Background

Acts 2, 41	The same day were added 3,000 souls.
Acts 2, 47	The Lord added daily to the Church such as should be saved.
Deuteronomy 11, 18–24	You shall therefore lay up these words of mine in your heart that your days may be multiplied.
Matthew 12, 25	A kingdom divided against itself is laid waste.
Acts 14, 4	The people of the city were divided.
Exodus 14, 21	The Lord divided the sea from the dry land.
Genesis 1	God divided the night from the day, the sea from the dry land.

11 Be worth your salt

Aim To demonstrate our responsibilities towards our fellow beings

Visual aids A packet of salt
Three cards with the words 'SALARIUM', 'SALT MONEY' and 'SALARY'

There was a buzz of excitement in the town, an air of expectancy. The news had just broken that the manager of the local football club had made a scoop. He had signed a football star from a foreign club. Everyone was expecting the club's fortunes to change dramatically. Great things were expected from the new star; he had a heavy burden to carry on his shoulders, a great responsibility. Everyone hoped he would rise to the occasion.

But things didn't quite work out right. The new, so-called star played in 12 matches and didn't score a single goal. In fact he didn't come near to scoring. The local team was bottom of the league. The fans soon started to demand that the new player should go because he 'wasn't worth his salt'.

Have you ever wondered what this phrase meant? It dates back to Roman times. Soldiers who faithfully served their emperor and country were rewarded with money, with which they could buy salt. This amount of money was called SALARIUM in Latin which translated means SALT MONEY. From the Latin word Salarium we get the modern English word SALARY. You see, salt is essential for health and fitness. Indeed we can't live without a certain amount of salt in our diet, though modern medical experts do say there is a danger of having too much salt as it could cause heart disease. The Roman soldiers knew that lack of salt would cause them to become weak, ineffective and generally in poor health.

You are probably looking forward to the time when you can leave school, get a job and start earning money. You may be paid a weekly wage or an annual salary which for convenience is divided into 12 equal monthly parts. A person's salary is really salt money. So a person who isn't worth his salt is not really deserving of his salary or wages.

Are you worth your salt? You will be if you try your hardest, realise your responsibilities and try to make your school an even better place. In this way you will be of real value.

Christian application

Jesus relies upon his followers to spread throughout the world the good news of the love of God. Before he ascended to Heaven he entrusted this task to his followers. Christian people should ask themselves if they are worth their salt. Are they trying to carry out Christ's wish to extend his kingdom of love in the world?

Reading   Mark 16, 14–16, 19–20
Hymn   'Go tell it on the mountain'

12 Fog

Aim   To encourage good order

Ask any motorist which weather condition he hates most and he will tell you *fog*. The motorist has to crawl along slowly, sometimes with his head out of the window because the beam from his headlamps seems to bounce back off the fog and dazzle the driver. When it is foggy, people become very confused, not knowing which way to turn, not being able to tell if they are wandering on to the wrong side of the road. Sadly, we often hear on the news of terrible accidents on the motorways because drivers have been driving too fast in fog, showing a total disregard for their own well-being and the safety of others.

The sensible thing for drivers to do in fog is to drive very carefully in convoy, keeping the rear lights of the vehicle in front just in view. If someone is ahead leading the way we somehow feel much safer.

Do you know of some people who behave as though they are in a fog? Give them a task to do and they seem to be bewildered, they don't know which way to turn, they don't know if they are heading in the right direction or they just blindly crash on ahead without much thought.

If ever we feel bewildered, confused and in a fog we would be well to follow the lead given by someone else, such as our parents, our teachers. Don't be reluctant to ask for help if you are in doubt. We must always be willing to accept good advice from those who have had more experience.

Christian application

When our way seems gloomy and we can't see our way through some particular dilemma we sometimes wish for a light to shine and disperse the gloom. We have such a light. For a start we have God's word: 'Thy word is a lamp to my feet and a light to my path' (Psalm 119, 105). God's word teaches us about Jesus, who said: 'I am the light of the world, he who follows me will not walk in darkness but will have the light of life' (John 8, 12). As we follow Jesus, who is the light, we must not neglect our duty to try ourselves to lighten the path for other people.

Reading   Matthew 5, 14–16
Prayer   18 or 20
Hymn   'God is love'

Prayers

1. O God our Father, we thank you for your love in sending your Son Jesus Christ to be our Saviour. Help us to trust him and to follow his example so that we need never be afraid.

2. We thank you Heavenly Father for the gift of your Son, our Saviour Jesus Christ. We thank you that Jesus died that we might be forgiven, that he died to make us good. Help us to show our gratitude by being kind and helpful to others, especially to all who are not as fortunate as we are.

3. Father in Heaven, help us to make the best use of our talents. May we all play our part in making this world a better place and in seeking to extend your kingdom of love.

4. Give us, O God, enquiring minds that, as we grow up, we may be able to find out the answers to important questions. In our work, may we never be afraid to ask questions and may we always be prepared to do our best. We thank you for all who teach us of your love. Help us always to be loving and kind to other people.

5. Heavenly Father, at this time of Advent help us to prepare ourselves for the coming of the Saviour into the world. Forgive us, we pray, for those times when we have been lazy, selfish, thoughtless, unkind; help us to be the sort of people you would have us to be. This we ask through Jesus Christ our Lord.

6. Help us, good Lord, to train our memories and to be orderly in our ways. May we never be forgetful but always remember and appreciate those who have helped us in so many different ways. May we show our gratitude by trying to be considerate and helpful to other people, both at school and at home.

7. Heavenly Father we ask that you will prosper the work of our school. May all those who serve you here, both teachers and pupils, always seek to do your will and do only that which would be pleasing in your sight. Grant that we ourselves, our country and your church shall be bettered by our studies because all shall be done to your praise and glory.

8   Father in Heaven, we remember in our prayers today, all those who have made sacrifices that we may enjoy peace and freedom. We thank you for all who gave their lives in order to make this world a better place. May their sacrifice not have been in vain but rather let us always show our appreciation by being concerned for others who are less fortunate than we are. 'They shall not grow old as we who are left grow old. Age shall not weary them or the years condemn. At the going down of the sun and in the morning we will remember them.'

9   Almighty God, accept our thanks, we pray, for all that the past year has meant to us: for the work we have done, for the lessons we have learned, for the pleasures we have enjoyed, for the friendships we have formed. May all that we have achieved remain with us and enrich our lives in the days to come.

10 Heavenly Father we come to you at the beginning of this new school year (term) to thank you for the holiday we have enjoyed and to ask for your help and blessing during the term which is just starting. Give us all the patience and determination we need to tackle new problems. Help us to be fair and considerate in all our dealings with other people. May we realise that we are now making good foundations for the rest of our lives.

11 *A prayer of St Patrick*
May the strength of God pilot us. May the power of God preserve us. May the wisdom of God instruct us. May the hand of God protect us. May the way of God direct us and may the shield of God defend us now and evermore.

12 O God our Heavenly Father help us, we pray, to live as you want us to live. Grant that we may always be truthful and kind, generous and considerate to those with whom we live and work, at home and at school. May we always be guided by your Holy Spirit and follow the teaching and example of our Lord Jesus Christ.

13 *A prayer by Dr William Barclay*
Today, O God, make me
Brave enough to face the things of which I am afraid;
Strong enough to overcome the temptations which try to make me do the wrong thing and not to do the right thing;

Persevering enough to finish every task that is given me to do;
Kind enough always to be ready to help others;
Obedient enough to obey your voice whenever you speak to me through my conscience;
Help me to live in purity; to speak in truth; to act in love all through to-day. This I ask for Jesus' sake.
                    Amen

14 O God our Father, make us aware of the work you have for us to do. Make us willing to do that work to the best of our ability. Help us to use our talents wisely and then may we know the joy that comes to all who serve you faithfully, through Jesus Christ our Lord. Amen.

15 Father in Heaven, we thank you for giving each of us the ability to do certain things well. May we always use our talents wisely in order to bring joy to others. Make us ready to dedicate ourselves and our talents to your service, so that your kingdom of love may be extended in the world around us, for the sake of Jesus Christ our Lord. Amen.

16 *A prayer by H Bisseker*
Help us this day, O God, to run with patience the race that is set before us. May neither opposition without nor discouragement within divert us from our goal. Inspire in us both strength of mind and steadfastness of purpose, that we may meet all fears and difficulties with unswerving courage and may fulfil with quiet fidelity the tasks committed to our charge; through Jesus Christ our Lord. Amen.

17 O Lord teach us, we pray, to live according to your rules. Make us trustworthy, honest, reliable and kind. Help us to keep our promises and to have faith in you. May we always seek to live following the example of our Lord Jesus Christ. Amen.

18 O Lord we pray that you will help us to be wise and sensible in all our ways. May we never act foolishly but rather seek to do your will in all things, relying upon your strength and the guidance of your Holy Spirit.

19 *A prayer by Dr William Barclay*
Help me today, O God,
To keep my temper and to control my tongue;
To keep my thoughts from wandering and my mind from straying;
To quarrel with no-one and to be friends with everyone.
So bring me to the end of today with nothing to be sorry for, and with nothing left undone, through Jesus Christ, Our Lord. Amen.

20 Grant us, Heavenly Father, the power of your Holy Spirit to strengthen us for the tasks we have to do each day. Grant us the guidance of your Holy Spirit when our way seems difficult. Grant us the inspiration of your Holy Spirit that we may know your will and seek to do it. May we always obey the promptings of your Spirit when you speak to us through our conscience. This we ask through Jesus Christ, Our Lord. Amen.

21 O God our Heavenly Father, we thank you for loving the world so much that you sent your son to be our Saviour. Help us to realise that it is through his death on the cross that we may be forgiven for the wrong we have done. May we show our gratitude by giving our love and service to Him who gave up everything for us, Jesus Christ, Our Lord. Amen.

22 Dear Father, as we give gifts to one another at Christmas time help us to remember that you gave the greatest gift of all to us, the gift of the Lord Jesus Christ who came to be our Saviour. May we show our gratitude by devoting our lives to your service and to the service of others.

23 We thank you, Heavenly Father, for the glorious tidings of Easter time, the good news that Jesus rose from the dead. We thank you, too, that His Spirit is still at work in the world today in the lives of all the people who love you. Help us to be guided by your Spirit to live the sort of lives you want us to live and follow the example of our Lord Jesus Christ. Amen.

24 Dear Lord, there are so many things for which we would like to thank you; for warm sunshine, refreshing rain, the beauty of nature, holiday times, our health and strength, our friends, our school, our homes and parents. So often we forget to thank you for these things and take them for granted.
   We pray that you will forgive us for the times when we have been thoughtless, selfish or lazy, when we have not shown our love for you by being helpful and kind to other people.

25 Loving Father, help us to be the sort of people you want us to be. We are sorry for the times when we have been selfish, lazy, greedy, jealous or dishonest. Forgive us, we pray, for our shortcomings and help us to become more like our Lord Jesus Christ.

26 We look around us day by day, Heavenly Father, and we see the evidence of your love for us in the world which you have created.

May we never take your goodness and providence for granted, but rather help us to show our appreciation in our service for you and for other people.

27 Dear Father, as another year passes beyond recall we look back with happy memories to those things we have enjoyed and to the times when we have been successful. Help us not to dwell too much upon our failings but rather to turn to the future with confidence, resolving to give of our best at all times, seeking in all things to do your will and trusting in you for strength.

28 *A prayer of St Ignatius Loyola*
Teach us good Lord to serve Thee as Thou desirest
To give and not to count the cost
To fight and not to heed the wounds
To toil and not to seek for rest
To labour and not to ask for any reward
Save that of knowing that we do Thy will.

29 Heavenly Father, help us to understand the message of Easter. We thank you that Jesus not only died but that he rose again so demonstrating your great love for us. Help us to know how he lives today in the hearts and lives of all who love and serve him. May we ourselves experience the true joy of Easter time.

30 Dear Father help us today to do nothing which would hurt other people, help us to say nothing which is untruthful or unkind, help us to avoid anything which is evil and to do only that which is good and so live this day as you would have us live.

31 Almighty God we pray especially today for all who are suffering because of the disaster at . . . . . . In particular we ask you to comfort and strengthen all who are in distress, so that they know the peace which you alone can give.

32 Loving Father we thank you for the wonderful world which you have created. As we look around us each day we can see the evidence of your love, for you have given us so many things to enjoy. May we always be careful not to do anything which would spoil your creation.

33 Heavenly Father we thank you for the excitement of Christmas time, for the love and friendship of our parents and relatives, and especially for your love in sending Jesus to be our Lord and Saviour. May the

spirit of goodwill at Christmas time last into the months which are ahead.

34 Dear Father, help us always to be aware of the needs of those people who are not as fortunate as we are, the poor, the sick, the aged, the lonely, the homeless and all who need a helping hand. Show us what we can do to help supply their needs and help them to know that there are those who care.

35 O God, we thank you especially today for all the people who have used their talents in the world of science and invention, to make this world a better, safer and happier place. Show us how we too may devote our small talents to the service of others. We ask this for the sake of him who gave his all for us, Jesus Christ our Lord.

36 Loving Father, as this new term begins we come to you to thank you for the holiday we have just enjoyed and to ask that you will be with us throughout this new school year, giving us new opportunities for learning and a desire to try our hardest, not only for our own sakes but for the good of others and for our school.

37 Heavenly Father, we are sorry that we sometimes fall short of the standards you set for us, that we sometimes hurt others by our words and deeds. Yet we thank you that you are a loving Father and pray that you will forgive us for anything we have done wrong and help us to be the sort of people you want us to be, for Jesus' sake.

38 O God our Father we thank you for the land in which we live and for all the people who make up our community. Help us all to work together in peace and harmony, using our skills and talents for the good of all, endeavouring at all times to make our country a happier place in which to live.

39 We thank you Heavenly Father for all we have been able to achieve throughout the term which is now drawing to a close. Help us to learn by any mistakes we have made and to be even more determined to give of our best next time. Protect us during the coming holidays that we may have a time of relaxation and enjoyment and so bring us safely to the beginning of a new term.

40 'All good gifts around us are sent from Heaven above, then thank the Lord, O thank the Lord for all His love'. Father, as we look around us day by day we see the evidence of your love for us. May

we never take your love for granted but always remember to thank you for your goodness and faithfulness.

41 Help us, O Lord, to make the most of the opportunities we are given each day, that we may give of our best in our work and in your service. Teach us how to use our knowledge and talents to help other people and show us how to be considerate and kind.

42 May God the Father bless us and all people everywhere and fill our hearts with his peace and goodwill.

43 May grace, mercy and peace from God the Father, God the Son and God the Holy Spirit, be with us all this day and always.

44 May the Lord grant us his blessing and fill our hearts with the spirit of truth and peace, now and evermore.

45 Now unto the King, eternal, immortal, invisible, the only wise God, be honour and glory for ever and ever.

46 The peace of God which passes all understanding, keep your hearts and minds through Jesus Christ our Lord.

47 The grace of the Lord Jesus Christ, the Love of God and the fellowship of the Holy Spirit be with us all now and for evermore. Amen.

Index

Abilities 6
accidents (avoiding) 47
advice 65, 73, 81, 84, 148
All Saints 12
anger 27
antiques 48
ants 70
appearance 105
appreciation 48, 72
asking questions 38
athletics 60
attention 94

Banquet 11
beauty 15
behaviour 25, 66, 75, 80, 96, 103
beware 94
birthday 20
boasting 73
boxing 58, 60

Career 26, 126
carelessness 75, 103
carols 24
cars 57
castles 2, 37
challenge 26
change 78
chemicals 15
children of Israel 4
Chinese 17
choices 26
Christian 86
Christmas 19, 20, 22, 24, 92
coldness 29, 53
colours 27, 29
cooking 5
communicating 65
concern 104, 137
conflicts 28
confusion 47, 50, 146
conscience 40
conscientiousness 105
conservation 137, 138
consideration 53, 105
consistency 129
courage 81
courtesy 48

cowardice 27
Cowdrey (Colin) 115
creation 39, 43, 54, 138
cricket 47, 115, 138
crooks 42
cross (the) 44
crossroads 81
crown (of life) 106
customs 22

Danger 27, 65, 80
death 132
decorations 23
dependence 73
despair 29
determination 3, 110, 129
differences 31, 130, 135
difficulties 65, 148
digging 104, 130
disasters 4, 18, 110, 129
disease 104, 136
disobedience 40, 43, 65, 80
disorder 50
divisions 145
doors 35
duty 69, 72, 136

Easter 40, 46, 114
effort 25
elections 89
encouragement 29
endings 131
environment 137, 138, 139
envy 27, 126
evil 100
examinations 3, 58, 61, 89, 110, 125, 129
excuses 10
example (of Jesus) 25, 42

Fair play 115
faith 96, 99, 110
fakes 130
famine 104, 136
Father Christmas 91
fighting 60, 136
fireworks 14
fishing 60

157

Index

flags 52, 65, 69
Flanders Field 16
fog 148
following Jesus 25, 60, 66, 76, 81, 86, 96, 105, 110, 142, 149
foolishness 45, 118
football 147
forecasts 89
forgiveness 29, 41, 43, 74, 108
foundations 2, 56
friends 64, 132
friendliness 65
fury 27

Generosity 91
give up 110
gloom 29
go 7
good example 76
Good Friday 100, 114
goodness 79
Good News 46, 148
Good Samaritan 7
gossip 103
gratitude 71
greatness 113
Great Supper 10
greed 108
guarantee 102
guidance 3
guilt 40

Hallmarks 48
Halloween 12
hands 31
happiness 14, 17, 107
harbour 68
hard work 45, 61, 70, 83, 86, 104, 105
harmony 77, 135
harvest 8, 71
hazards 65, 80
help/helpfulness 6, 19, 25, 29, 34, 42, 65, 73, 83, 93
Highway Code 80
holidays 131
Holy Spirit 4, 52
home 37, 104
homework 10, 25, 33, 105, 111, 115, 118
honesty 48, 108, 115, 124
hope 29

humility 113
Hunt (William Holman) 36

Ice 94
ignorance 137
importance 5, 75, 76
impurities 108
Isaac Newton 35

Janus 93
jealousy 108, 113, 126
jewels 130
Joshua 26
journey 80

Kindness 19, 29, 53, 79, 96, 127
knowledge 56

Ladders 3, 125
Lake District 70
Lamb of God 100
Laziness 32, 65, 80, 108, 125
learning 38
letters 101
light 14, 22, 149
listening 107
lost property 142
Love of God 3, 38, 39, 43, 55, 72, 132
luck 3

Magnificat 19
magnifying 19
Mary, Mother of Jesus 19
materialism 17
memory 16, 111
mince pies 23
mistakes 25, 137, 140
mistletoe 22
modesty 113
morality 96
music 107, 116, 135

Names 66, 85, 87
neighbourliness 39, 47, 105, 136
Nelson, Admiral Lord 69
new school year 2, 25, 64
nicknames 85
noise 14

Obedience 107, 115
opportunities 93

order 50, 70, 148

Pagan customs 22
parables 10, 107
parties 20
peacemakers 117, 144
persevere 3
pilot 66
pleasure 14
poppies 16
possessions 17, 37, 45
poverty 104, 137
praying 66, 105, 128
preparation 89, 104, 118
priorities 42
privacy 37
prizes 60
problems 116, 131
procrastination 33
promises 9, 25, 29, 52, 143
prophecies 89
providence 72
provocation 14
punctuality 86, 105, 115
purity 29, 96, 102

Quarrelling 50, 116, 122, 132, 146

Radio 65
readiness 7
regret 80
reliability 48, 86, 93, 144
remembering 16, 72, 94, 105, 108, 142
Remembrance Day 16
reputations 25, 93
respect 37, 79, 136
responsibilities 10, 69, 103, 142, 147
resurrection 46, 114
retaliation 66
reward 32, 56, 61
rice 17
right living 7
roots 100
ruins 37
rules 47, 105
rust 57

Sailing 52
Saints 12
salt 147
sand 54

Santa Claus 91
savings 61
Saviour 88, 92, 105
seaside 2
seeds 8
selfishness 108
Sermon on the Mount 18
setbacks 110, 125
sharing 122, 145
sheep 142
Sherlock Holmes 19
ships 65, 69
shortcomings 58
signals 7
silence 29, 83
sincerity 101
singlemindedness 60
Solomon (King) 70
Sower (parable of) 107
sport (teams) 5, 50, 110, 125, 138
Spring 114
standards 58
stars 55
stealing 28
stop 7, 66, 80
storms 2
success 70, 93, 107, 125, 126
suffering 38, 100
superstitions 4, 12, 22
surroundings 64

Talents 8, 31, 116, 135
teamwork 5, 50
television 65, 105, 131, 136
temper 14, 25, 66, 113, 142
temperance 96
temptation 57, 65, 81, 104, 127
tennis 110, 138
theft 37
Third World 134
thoughtlessness 86
time 83
tolerance 133
Trafalgar (battle of) 69
treasure 37
trees 137
tricks 45
Trinity 4
trivialities 56
trusting 9
truthfulness 48, 108, 113, 115, 124

Understanding 133
Universe 54

Value 48, 130
vandalism 80
victory 104

War 16, 28, 38, 103, 104, 143
warnings 80, 94, 141
warm personality 29
water 138
Way (the) 35
weather 89, 138
wedding 118

welcome 2, 64
Whitsuntide 52, 120
wind 52
wisdom 56, 70, 83
Wise Men 23
wishing 23
Word of God 148
work 45, 61, 70, 83, 86, 104, 125, 145
world 6, 8, 42, 100, 104
worry 7
worship 106
wrongdoing 29, 81